Withdrawn

ARTS, LEISURE, AND SPORT IN ANCIENT EGYPT

DON NARDO

LUCENT BOOKS

An imprint of Thomson Gale, a part of The Thomson Corporation

THOMSON

GALE

Detroit • New York • San Francisco • San Diego • New Haven, Conn. • Waterville, Maine • London • Munich

© 2005 Thomson Gale, a part of The Thomson Corporation.

Thomson and Star Logo are trademarks and Gale and Lucent Books are registered trademarks used herein under license.

For more information, contact
Lucent Books
27500 Drake Rd.
Farmington Hills, MI 48331-3535
Or you can visit our Internet site at http://www.gale.com

LIBRARY OF CONGRESS CATALOGING-IN-PUBLICATION DATA

Nardo, Don, 1947–
  Arts, leisure, and sport in ancient Egypt / by Don Nardo.
    p. cm. — (The Lucent library of historical eras)
  Includes bibliographical references and index.
  ISBN 1-59018-706-7 (hard cover : alk. paper)
  1. Egypt—Social life and customs—To 332 B.C.—Juvenile literature. 2. Arts, Egyptian—Juvenile literature. 3. Leisure—Egypt—History—To 1500—Juvenile literature. 4. Sports—Egypt—History—To 1500—Juvenile literature. I. Title. II. Series: Lucent library of historical eras. Ancient Egypt.
DT61.N3275 2005
700'.932—dc22
                                                                    2004030542

Printed in the United States of America

Contents

Foreword

Looking back from the vantage point of the present, history can be viewed as a myriad of intertwining roads paved by human events. Some paths stand out—broad highways whose mileposts, even from a distance of centuries, are clear. The events that propelled the rise to power of Germany's Third Reich, its role in World War II, and its eventual demise, for example, are well defined and documented.

Other roads are less distinct, their route sometimes hidden from view. Modern legislatures may have developed from old tribal councils, for example, but the links between them are indistinct in places, open to discussion and interpretation.

The architecture of civilization—law, religion, art, science, and government—as well as the more everyday aspects of our culture—what we eat, what we wear—all developed along the historical roads and byways. In that progression can be traced through every facet of modern life.

A broad look back along these roads reveals that many paths—though of vastly different character—seem to converge at a few critical junctions. These intersections are those great historical eras that echo over the long, steady course of human history, extending beyond the past and into the present.

These epic periods of time are the focus of Lucent's Library of Historical Eras. They shine through the mists of history like beacons, illuminated by a burst of creativity that propels events forward—so bright that we, from thousands of years away, can clearly see the chain of events leading to the present.

Each Lucent Library of Historical Eras consists of a set of books that highlight various aspects of these major eras. For example, the Elizabethan England library features volumes on Queen Elizabeth I and her court, Elizabethan theater, the great playwrights, and everyday life in Elizabethan London.

The mini-library approach allows for the division of each era into its most significant and most interesting parts and the exploration of those parts in depth. Also, social and cultural trends as well as illustrative documents and eyewitness accounts can be prominently featured in individual volumes.

Lucent's Library of Historical Eras presents a wealth of information to young readers. The lively narrative, fully documented primary and secondary source quotations, maps, photographs, sidebars, and annotated bibliographies serve as launching points for class discussion and further research.

In studying the great historical eras, students also develop a better understanding of our own times. What we learn from the past and how we apply it in the present may shape the future and may determine whether our era will be a guiding light to those traveling future roads.

Introduction

The Structured Lives of Egyptian Craftsmen

Today books and articles about ancient Egypt often mention or discuss art and artists. However, these are simply convenient terms designed to make ancient Egyptian society and people more understandable to modern readers. The truth is that the Egyptians had neither the concept nor a word for *artist* in the modern sense—that is, a creatively gifted person whom society singles out for his or her achievements. Instead, Egypt had craftsmen, men (and occasionally women) who were skilled at making things. There were gifted individuals among them, just as there are today, of course. But such individuals rarely, if ever, achieved the status, fame, and wealth that successful modern artists enjoy.

This is mainly because ancient Egyptian craftsmen occupied a more or less set and rigid position on the social ladder. This position was higher than that of ordinary peasants and laborers, who performed unskilled, menial work. But it was decidedly lower than the social level of the nobles and wealthy elite, who made up the smallest but most powerful sector of society. At their own leisure, and to serve their own needs, the elites employed the craftsmen and rewarded them for their work. But the rewards usually took the form of necessities such as food and shelter. The elites did not view craftsmen as their equals and discouraged and prevented craftsmen from climbing the social ladder past the modest rungs traditionally allotted to them.

Perpetuating the Status Quo

Tradition, more than skill or any other single factor, governed the lives of Egyptian craftsmen, as well as other members of Egyptian society, from the lowliest peasant to the mightiest pharaoh. Egypt had one of the most rigidly traditional and unchanging societies in the ancient world. Though the Greeks and Romans cherished their own traditions and maintained some of them for many centuries, Greek and Roman societies underwent numerous and often profound social, religious, and artistic changes. In contrast, with a few minor exceptions, the ancient Egyptians maintained roughly the same religious practices, social customs, and artistic styles and conventions for nearly three thousand years.

One of the major factors in this strong emphasis on tradition and fixed social structure was geography. Egyptian civilization evolved within a unique geographical niche that over time deeply affected the character and worldview of the people of the Nile Valley. Most Egyptians lived on a narrow, fertile strip of land running north to south along the shores of the Nile, one of the world's major rivers. Beyond this populated strip stretched many miles of arid deserts. These wastelands created a formidable natural barrier that for many centuries kept the populated regions of Egypt more or less isolated (as well as insulated) from the outside world. The result was that the Egyptians came to see their land as the center of the world and themselves and their traditional ways as superior to those of foreigners. Outsiders and their social and artistic customs were viewed as inferior, backward, and not to be emulated.

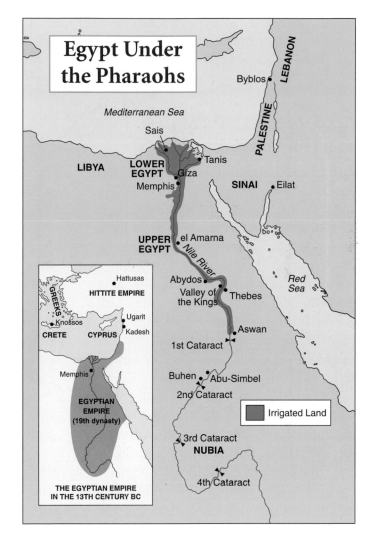

For inspiration, therefore, the Egyptians turned inward and venerated and perpetuated the status quo. As Egyptologist Joyce Tyldesley explains:

Egypt's geography encouraged an innate conservatism that manifested itself in a highly distinctive and decidedly self-restrained culture. The visual arts proved particularly resistant to change, with Egypt's painters and sculptors looking backwards rather than outwards, rejecting foreign influences and seeking instead inspiration from their country's past.[1]

Accepted Artistic Styles and Conventions

Egyptian craftsmen likewise perpetuated the status quo: The country's artistic styles and conventions changed little throughout Egypt's major ancient ages (as formulated by modern scholars). These include the Old Kingdom (ca. 2686–2181 B.C.), during which most of Egypt's pyramids were built; the Middle Kingdom (ca. 2055–1650 B.C.), in which the Egyptians began expanding their territory by conquest; and the New Kingdom (ca. 1550–1069 B.C.), in which a series of strong pharaohs built an Egyptian empire. (There were several other eras before, between, and after the big three, including the last two, spanning the years 332 B.C. to A.D. 395, during which first Greeks and then Romans ruled Egypt.)

One obvious way that Egyptian craftsmen maintained the artistic status quo during most of these centuries was through uniform depictions of the human body. Even before the advent of the Old Kingdom, they began to employ what modern scholars call "canons of proportion." These were essentially artistic rules, patterns, and measurements designed to make all painted and sculpted figures look basically alike. In the most prevalent example, a painter sketched a grid containing eighteen squares, each square measuring the size of the painter's fist; he then sketched a human form within the rigid confines of the grid.

Painters and other craftsmen were guided and constrained by other artistic traditions besides the canons of proportion. Whether in paintings or sculptures, for example, human bodies were almost always shown in set, very formal, and somewhat stilted and peculiar poses. According to noted scholar Ian Shaw, the craftsmen

portrayed each individual element of the subject from the most representative angle. The human torso and eye were clearly best both viewed from the front, whereas the arms, leg, and face were best seen from the side. This concern with separate components at the expense of the overall effect often causes Egyptian depictions of human figures to appear distorted and internally inconsistent to modern eyes.[2]

This odd convention of mixing front views of the torso and eye with profiles of the head and legs is often called frontalism.

Another accepted convention that was more idealistic and symbolic than realistic was using the size of a human figure to emphasize the importance of the individual depicted. In royal paintings and statues, for instance, the pharaoh was always by far the largest figure. The figures of his wives and children were much smaller, and his enemies were smaller still and depicted as kneeling or otherwise groveling before him. Egyptian craftsmen were expected to follow these and other artistic conventions

In this reenactment staged for a television documentary, ancient Egyptian artists utilize grids to give their subjects proper proportions.

and rules. And there was little room for personal, creative innovation.

Life in the Workers' Villages

Egyptian craftsmen also perpetuated accepted tradition through the structure of their daily lives, which was dictated largely by their social status and the needs and rules of their wealthy, elite employers. When a pharaoh needed a temple or tomb built, for example, the call went out for stonemasons, sculptors, painters, carpenters, goldsmiths, and other craftsmen. Such skilled laborers usually had little choice but to answer the call.

These workers also often had no choice in where to live. The work sites were chosen by the pharaoh and his architects, and the craftsmen and laborers working on the project had to move to temporary villages set up nearby. The unearthed remains of a few such workers' villages constitute one of the main sources of information about Egyptian craftsmen. (Other sources include depictions of craftsmen in paintings on the walls of wealthy tombs; administrative lists of craft professions and their wages; and the surviving remains of the works created by the craftsmen.) Perhaps the most famous excavated workers' village is the one at Deir el-Medina on the Nile's west bank

Ancient mud-brick walls rise near Luxor, on the Nile's west bank. The ruins of the workers' village at Deir el-Medina can be seen in the background.

near the Valley of the Kings, the desolate, rocky area where many of the pharaohs of the New Kingdom placed their tombs. The craftsmen who built, decorated, and outfitted these tombs lived in Deir el-Medina. A similar village was unearthed in the 1990s near the great pyramids on the Giza plateau (near modern Cairo).

The remains of such workers' villages show the size and layout of the houses (which were modest but larger and better furnished than peasants' huts), the kinds of food eaten by the inhabitants, their religious customs and burials, and so forth. The ruins also indicate how structured, rigid, and sometimes even secluded their lives could be. These towns, English Egyptologist A. Rosalie David points out,

were built to a predetermined plan.... There was a brick enclosure wall that confined the workmen and their families to a particular location. The sites were all on the desert's edge, chosen because of proximity to the royal burial site and also because isolation ensured that their inhabitants (who had knowledge of the location and construction of the tombs) could be guarded. They were enclosed communities that were allowed as little contact as possible with the outside world.[3]

Even during their leisure time, which must have been limited, the craftsmen, along with most other Egyptians, followed accepted social traditions and structure. People invariably played the same sports and games their ancestors played, and they hunted and fished for the same animals, using traditional, tried-and-true weapons and methods.

Balancing Work and Play

Repetition and tradition are not necessarily boring or repressive concepts, however.

That the ancient Egyptians were tradition-bound does not mean that they were downtrodden, somber, or unhappy people. In fact, evidence suggests that strong adherence to tradition gave people peace of mind and a sense of security.

The key seems to have been to find a means of relaxation and pleasure within the guidelines of a highly structured lifestyle. And this the Egyptians managed to do. As Brooklyn Museum scholar James Romano puts it, they were "a fun-loving people who filled their leisure hours with pleasant diversions." They balanced work and play rather skillfully and effectively, despite the restrictions society placed on their status, living conditions, and modes of artistic and personal expression. "Their lives were certainly ordered," says Romano, "but we never sense that they felt constrained by their rules and traditions. The Egyptians loved life and hoped to perpetuate its most pleasant aspects in the hereafter."[4]

Chapter One

ARTISTRY IN STONE

Among the earliest of the artistic skills mastered by ancient Egyptian craftsmen were those in which they manipulated one of nature's basic materials—stone. In fact, during Egypt's Neolithic Age (or New Stone Age, ca. 9000–5500 B.C.[5]), long before towns or kingdoms had risen in the area, the primitive inhabitants made sophisticated stone tools. Later, during the Predynastic Period (ca. 5500–3100 B.C.), they learned to create bowls, vases, and other vessels from stone. These were made for ordinary functional use. Yet as surviving examples attest, many had aesthetic quality (artistic beauty) as well as practical value.

In the late Predynastic Period (beginning perhaps about 3400 B.C.) and on into the Early Dynastic Period (ca. 3100–2686 B.C.) and Old Kingdom, the Egyptians learned to build with stone. The first monumental, or large-scale, structures that architects and stonemasons designed and erected were rectangular tombs known as mastabas. These evolved into the first stone pyramid tombs. In the early years of the Old Kingdom the largest pyramids of all (those of the pharaohs Khufu, Khafre, and Menkaure) were built on the Giza plateau, near modern Cairo. Skilled stonemasons also played key roles in constructing temples, palaces, obelisks, forts, and other monumental stone structures.

Another group of artists working with stone were the sculptors who decorated the insides (and sometimes the outsides) of tombs, palaces, and other buildings. Some specialized in carving reliefs (or bas-reliefs), three-dimensional figures and scenes raised from a flat background (usually a wall) but still attached to it. Such reliefs depicted a wide range of subjects, from small vignettes of personal life to giant battle scenes in which the pharaohs triumphed over their enemies. Other sculptors carved freestanding statues ranging in size from tiny figurines only a few inches tall to gigantic images weighing hundreds of tons.

The big ones are generally referred to as "colossi," from the word *colossal*.

Making Stone Tools

Long before production of such large stone reliefs and statues began, Egyptian craftsmen had mastered the skills needed to make stone tools, which for thousands of years were the only tools available. Among these were stone knives with straight or S-shaped backs and curved cutting edges. Other common stone tools included oblong axes and saw blades for cutting wood; long, curved sickles for harvesting wheat; fist-sized scrapers for preparing animal hides; and weapons such as battle-axes, spearheads, and arrowheads.

The most common method of making such tools and weapons, especially before the Old Kingdom, was knapping, or chipping. Artisans used a piece of very hard

The remains of a number of ancient mastabas surround the imposing Step Pyramid at Sakkara, the tomb of the pharaoh Djoser.

stone, such as basalt or dolerite, to chip and thereby shape and sharpen a piece of softer stone, such as jasper. The majority of stone blades were made of jasper, chert, or flint. A number of scenes painted on the walls of tombs show craftsmen employing this technique. Charles University scholar Eugen Strouhal describes such a scene found in a Middle Kingdom tomb at Beni Hasan (about 125 miles south of Cairo):

> A craftsman can be seen holding a roughly shaped knife-blade in one hand and in the other a stake-like tool with a point evidently made of specially hard stone, set at an angle in a cylindrical wooden handle. He is using delicate pressure to dress the blade, chipping small fragments from its surface and sharpening its cutting edge.[6]

A supplementary technique was to hone and further sharpen a stone blade by rubbing it with a piece of sandstone, which acted like sandpaper.

Although metal tools largely replaced stone ones in the Old, Middle, and New kingdoms, some stone tools remained in use throughout the country's history. Most of these were retained for age-old rituals; this is not surprising, since the Egyptians were such sticklers for maintaining tradition. For example, after vis-

iting Egypt in the fifth century B.C., long after the close of the New Kingdom, the Greek historian Herodotus reported that local embalmers still used ritual flint knives to open the abdomens of corpses. Similarly, priests continued to use stone knives to slaughter animals during sacrifices. And very sharp stone blades remained the preferred tool for performing circumcisions.

This stone panel in Cairo's Egyptian Museum shows workmen using stone tools to carve a statue.

The Art of Stone Vessels

The next stone-working skill mastered by Egyptian artisans was making stone vessels, an industry the ancient Egyptians raised to a virtual art. Vessels included cups, bowls, plates, vases, pitchers, trays, containers for storing oils and incense, and canopic jars (containers that held the internal organs removed from a body during mummification). In fact, practically every kind of vessel that the ancients later made from pottery or metal was first made in Egypt from stone.

The first step in making such a container was to locate suitable materials. Most stone vessels were made from relatively soft kinds of stone, such as limestone, sandstone, or alabaster. Softer material was obviously easier to shape than harder stone such as quartz or granite; vessels of such hard stones were thus rare and expensive.

The second step was to fashion the outside of the vessel. A craftsman did this by pounding the stone's surface with a hard stone ball or a small, blunt stone pick. Sandstone or other abrasive materials were employed to smooth and polish the outer surfaces.

The final step—hollowing out the vessel's interior—was the most difficult and time-consuming one. Classical scholar Lionel Casson provides this clear description of the process:

> The scooping out of the interior . . . [was done] with the aid of some abrasive, such as quartz sand, which is harder than most stone and will abrade [grind down] even stone of the same hardness, just as diamond dust will cut diamonds. Vases that were cylindrical could be scooped out by endless drilling, with the [drill] bit turned in wetted fine quartz sand, the sand doing the actual cutting. The craftsmen's skill was so accomplished that they were able to leave the walls of a vase paper-thin, no more than a millimeter in thickness.[7]

Stonemasonry

Once wealthy ancient Egyptians began to commission monumental stone structures, some stone-tool and stone-vessel makers began to specialize in another area—masonry. These artisans used some of the same methods that had been perfected for vessel making, adapting them to the larger scale required for erecting walls and buildings. For example, the surface of a stone wall block was first roughly shaped by pounding it with a hard stone ball or pick. From the Middle Kingdom on, copper or bronze picks were also used, especially on softer stones like limestone and sandstone.

The next step was dressing, or smoothing and refining, the surface of a building stone. Egyptian masons soon learned that this time-consuming step was not necessary for every stone. Only a structure's outer stones, those visible to the eye or those that needed to fit precisely, required such dressing. It became quite common in some structures, therefore, to create a sort of shell of outer dressed stones and to line the interior of the shell with roughly hewn stone. (In freestanding defensive walls or the outer walls of fortresses

Modern reenactors portray ancient Egyptian sculptors at work. The man in the foreground uses a wooden hammer to strike a metal chisel.

or palaces, the shell was sometimes filled with rubble.) The great pyramids at Giza are a prominent example. With a few exceptions only the outer layers of stone blocks in these structures were dressed, while the inner sides of the solid walls remained rough-hewn. To dress the outer surface of a rough-hewn stone block, masons trimmed excess material using copper or bronze saws and chisels. (They pounded the chisels with wooden mallets of various sizes.) Then they used a piece of sandstone to grind down smaller irregularities.

The surfaces of some stones, such as those that lined the interior walls of a palace and would be painted, needed to be as flat and flawless as possible. Stonemasons frequently tested and corrected the degree of flatness of these stones as they worked. According to Dieter Arnold, an authority on ancient building methods, they applied red paint to a wooden board and carefully pressed the board onto the surface of the block. "The color would stick to the protruding areas," he says,

which then had to be treated again. . . . Another tool, which probably was more frequently used, was the boning rod. Two equally long rods were connected at their tops by a string that could thus be stretched [with the rods held vertically] over the surface to be tested. A third rod of the same length [also held vertically] could be held under the string [and run back and forth over the stone's surface]. . . . If there still [were] protruding parts, the third rod would show above the line of the string [and a mason would use a hammer and chisel to chop off the protruding parts].[8]

Stone Sculptures: Reliefs

Copper, bronze, and occasionally stone chisels, saws, and drills were also used to produce the magnificent stone reliefs that graced the walls of many Egyptian temples and palaces. These carved scenes reached their height of complexity and beauty in the New Kingdom.

The first steps in creating a big relief involved careful planning and sketching, so the artisans involved had to be skilled draftsmen as well as carvers. One or more supervisors decided on the composition of the scene, including how the registers would be arranged. A register was a horizontal panel or band of reliefs (or paintings); a complete composition might include a single register or several, one placed above another, on a wall.

Following accepted conventions, the arrangement of the registers, as well as the size of the figures in the relief, told the viewer a story in a chronological sequence. Egyptologist Jaromir Malek explains:

The lowest register on the wall was regarded as chronologically the latest; within the register, the episode closest to the [largest] figure [most often the pharaoh or some other important person] . . . was the most recent. The scenes in registers were oriented towards the large figure. Each scene was then designed by deciding on details such as the number of people to be shown and how.[9]

Once the subject and placement of figures were decided, artisans began applying preliminary sketches to the wall, which first had been smoothed with plaster. Using red paint, they drew rough outlines of figures and objects. They made sure to follow the prevailing canon of proportions, the set of rules defining the proper depiction of the human form. (During the Old Kingdom, three or four general guidelines per figure were sufficient; in the Middle Kingdom, a more involved system using a grid of squares came into use.) When the draftsmen were finished with the sketches, the supervisors added any needed corrections in black ink. Finally, the artisans used their chisels and other tools to chip away stone in appropriate spots to create the raised relief. The finished products were then painted in bright colors.

In large-scale reliefs in palaces and other major structures, the proper placement of registers, the depiction of varying-sized figures, the choice of colors, and other conventions combined to tell onlookers a specific and often dramatic story. One of the most impressive surviving examples is

A Great Battle Commemorated in Stone

Among the finest surviving stone sculptures of ancient Egypt is a series of battle reliefs on the walls of the palaces and temples of the New Kingdom pharaohs. One of the most impressive was commissioned by Ramesses III in his mortuary temple at Medinet Habu (near Thebes) to commemorate his victory over the Sea Peoples, who attacked the Nile Delta. In this tract from his book The Collapse of the Bronze Age, *scholar Manuel Robbins describes the scene depicted in the relief.*

A fortified doorway at Medinet Habu features sculpted scenes of Ramesses III defeating his enemies.

The Sea Battle sculptural relief . . . is about 55 feet wide. . . . Here, represented in a compressed composition . . . was a clash which occurred on the water somewhere near shore. . . . On the right stands the pharaoh . . . launching shafts [arrows] at the enemy from his unerring bow. Stretching across the bottom of the illustration are Egyptian soldiers, marching off with Sea Peoples prisoners. On the left is the battle on the water. . . . Here there is a clash among ships . . . [which] are arranged in three rows [registers], one above the other. In each row there are three ships. Three along the left and one on the lower right are manned by Egyptians, and the rest are those of the Sea Peoples. . . . The scene shows a fierce mêlée of close combat. Egyptian boats have their oars out so that they are able to maneuver, but in the Sea Peoples boats, oars are shipped [pulled inside the vessels]. They are unable to maneuver. They have been caught by surprise it seems. . . . [The] Sea Peoples are in disarray, drowned, dead. The water is filled with them.

a relief created by the craftsmen of the noted warrior-pharaoh Ramesses II (reigned ca. 1279–1213 B.C.). Located at Luxor, a temple complex on the east bank of the Nile near ancient Thebes, the relief celebrated Ramesses' victory over the Hittites (a people from Asia Minor, what is now Turkey) at Kadesh, in Syria. "The Kadesh sculpture at Luxor is a masterpiece of composition and clarity," scholar Manuel Robbins writes.

> It was necessary to show each of the groups who participated in the battle in such a way that the onlooker would instantly recognize each. . . . In the left center the viewer sees the fortress of Kadesh, with battlements and towers. . . . Just outside the fortress [warriors] are assembled. . . . Distinct nationalities are evident. Hittites can be recognized by their hairstyle . . . Syrians by their long hair, beards, and robes, and other nationalities by long braided hair. . . . In the right center is Ramesses in his chariot, facing Kadesh. He is superhuman in size, towering over ordinary mortals. . . . At the far left is a figure of larger than ordinary size, yet much smaller than Ramesses. . . . His chariot is faced away from the action, as if a quick escape is contemplated. This is how the Egyptians present Muwatallis, the Hittite king. In the center of the composition . . . is a scene of chaotic battle. Hittite chariots and horses are overturned. Bodies, all of them Hittite or Hittite allies, are tumbling through the air. . . . [This] massive slaughter . . . is the story in pictures as Ramesses wanted it told.[10]

This illustration created for a modern book about Egypt is based on stone reliefs showing Ramesses II fighting the Hittites at Kadesh.

The Biggest Statue in Egypt

Of the many colossi erected in ancient Egypt, the so-called Great Sphinx at Giza was the largest. Originally, its facial features were based on those of Khafre, the pharaoh who commissioned the statue. (It was part of the complex of buildings and statues surrounding Khafre's pyramid, the second biggest on the Giza plateau.) The statue's head featured a pleated headdress, the *names*, which is still largely intact. Gone, however, are a cobra (a symbol associated with royalty) above the forehead and a false beard, both of which fell off or were smashed in ancient times. The nose is also missing. The Great Sphinx is about 66 feet high and 240 feet long. It was carved mainly out of low-quality limestone, part of a rocky outcrop that existed on the plateau before people started building there. Some ruins located directly in front of the statue are those of a small temple (appropriately called the Sphinx Temple) that once stood on that spot.

The Great Sphinx at Giza, depicting the pharaoh Khafre, is now missing its nose and a number of other details.

Stone Sculptures: Statues

The artisans who worked with stone also produced numerous freestanding statues. Many were fashioned for the interiors (and sometimes the exteriors) of tombs; others stood inside and outside of temples, palaces, and other monumental structures. Some statues depicted gods and goddesses, others humans.

Those statues representing people more or less captured the actual physical attributes of their subjects. This was partly because most statues were viewed as potential host vehicles for the spirits of the deceased. It was thought that a spirit could enter and rest in a statue and from it communicate with living people. The more the statue looked like the dead person, the more likely the spirit could use the host vehicle. Thus the artisans who sculpted the many surviving statues of Ramesses II did their best to capture his features.

Egyptian statues were carved from wood, metal, and stone. Most of the surviving statues are of stone, mainly because most of the wooden ones have rotted away and most of the metal ones were melted down in late ancient and medieval times. A wide variety of stone was used, including limestone, alabaster, sandstone, obsidian, calcite, serpentine, granite, and basalt. Noted Egyptologist Gay Robins explains the typical building process:

A statue began as a rectangular block of stone slightly larger than the desired size of the finished object [because a certain amount of stone would be removed during the carving process].

Front and back views of the image were sketched out on the front and back of the block, while profile images were drawn on each of the sides. From the Middle Kingdom on, these outlines were probably laid out on a squared grid [following the prevailing canon of proportion] . . . that ran all the way around the block so as to ensure that all the sketches matched up. Sculptors then cut away the stone on all four sides and the top around the sketched outline until they achieved the rough shape of the statue. As they cut the sketch . . . away with the [discarded] stone, they would re-mark important levels and points with lines or dots of paint. Once they had the outline of the statue shaped, they could concentrate on modeling the face and body and executing the details of costume.[11]

The amount of time and effort involved in this process naturally depended on the size of the statue. Many Egyptian statues were life-size or smaller. But some were colossi of enormous proportions, requiring the contributions of dozens or even hundreds of artisans and supporting laborers (who did the menial quarrying, lifting, and dragging). Two stone colossi erected by the New Kingdom pharaoh Amenhotep III (ca. 1390–1352 B.C.), for example, are more than 50 feet high and weigh more than 700 tons each. These were surpassed by one of Ramesses II's giant statues, which was 62 feet tall and weighed some 1,000 tons. Ramesses' artisans then outdid themselves by creating four colossi for the front façade of his great

Conventional Poses for Statues

A few general styles and poses of human statues evolved during the Old Kingdom and, as scholar Jaromir Malek says in his book about Egyptian art, these "continued to be used for the rest of Egyptian history." In the following excerpt, he describes some conventional poses.

[M]any statues] show a seated figure, and this type remained most frequent for the next two thousand years. One of the hands usually rests flat on the knee, while the other is clenched in a fist. The second main type, the standing figure, also appeared early. The man is usually standing upright, with his gaze fixed in the distance, his left foot advanced . . . his hands held alongside the body with the fists clenched. The third type, the scribe statue, was introduced during the Fourth Dynasty, around 2540 b.c. . . . It shows [a] deceased [person] seated on the ground with his legs crossed in the typical posture of an Egyptian scribe. . . . Other types of statue, for example kneeling figures, were very rare.

One of several large statues of Amenhotep III at Luxor shows him in a conventional pose.

temple at Abu Simbel (about 170 miles south of Aswan, in southern Egypt). These enormous figures are 72 feet high and may weigh as much as 1,500 tons each. The only statue created in ancient Egypt bigger than these is the famous Sphinx at Giza, which is about 66 feet high and 240 feet long. These monuments will likely continue to stand for thousands of years more, awe-inspiring testimony to the talents of long-vanished craftsmen who executed true artistry in stone.

Chapter Two

PRODUCTION OF POTTERY AND GLASS

After stone tools, weapons, and containers, among the earliest items produced by Egyptian craftsmen were those made of pottery, or ceramics. There were two basic types of ancient Egyptian ceramics. The first, and by far the most abundant, was common pottery made from the mud (or silt or clay) laid down each year by the Nile River. Modern scholars refer to it as coarse ware or Nile silt ware. The potters made bowls, cups, dishes, jugs, wine jars, oil flasks, vases, lamps (that burned oil), canopic jars, statuettes for tombs, and many other practical and generally inexpensive objects.

Partly because these products were common and cheap, coarse ware potters, like most other Egyptian artisans, achieved only a minimal degree of social status and respect. In fact, the Egyptian name for potters, *kedu,* was the same term applied to mud-brick makers, who were widely viewed as lowly, unskilled laborers. (This was probably because both groups worked with mud.) In a Middle Kingdom document, a man named Khety admonishes his son to get an education so that he will not have to become an ordinary laborer. Khety states with disdain:

The potter is covered all over with earth, though he is still among the living. He has to grub in it like a pig or worse so that he can fire [bake] the pots. His muddy clothes are in tatters. He breathes in through his nose the air that comes out of the oven.[12]

Another reason for potters' low status was that their products were generally of lesser quality than those of many other Egyptian craftsmen. At least this was true throughout most of pharaonic times (that is, during the centuries Egyptian pharaohs ruled the country). During most of these centuries, Egyptian pottery did not achieve the artistic excellence of pottery in other Mediterranean regions, especially Greece.

These painted wooden statuettes from the Middle Kingdom show potters preparing to bake their wares in an open kiln fueled by wood.

The quality of Egyptian pottery was better in the Predynastic Period, particularly between 5500 and 4000 B.C., and toward the end of pharaonic times, after the influx of Greek influences and eventually Greek settlers into Egypt from the sixth to the first century B.C. (Scholars refer to the important Egyptian era lasting from 332 to 30 B.C. as the Ptolemaic Period, named after Ptolemy, a Greek general who became pharaoh and whose descendants made up Egypt's last pharaonic dynasty.)

The other major category of Egyptian pottery was faience. Made from stone dust rather than mud, it produced wares that were higher in quality, more expensive, and more in demand among the upper classes. Another craft product made from crushed stone—glass—enjoyed only a brief period of popularity in pharaonic times (during the New Kingdom). But glassmaking reemerged in Ptolemaic times and thereafter remained one of Egypt's most important crafts.

Making Coarse Ware

Long before glassmaking evolved, Egyptian potters were turning out coarse ware for people's everyday use. The first step in the process of making this form of pottery was to prepare the clay by kneading it. This was most often accomplished by trampling—that is, walking—on a large batch of clay with one's bare feet. Surviving wall paintings showing potters at work indicate that smaller batches were sometimes kneaded by hand. During this step, the potter added chopped straw and/or animal dung to reduce the clay's stickiness.

The next step was to shape the kneaded clay into the form desired. This was done completely by hand until sometime between 3000 and 2400 B.C. Scholars differ widely on the exact date that the first potter's wheel appeared in Egypt. Whenever it was, primitive early versions required the artisan to turn the wheel with his left hand while shaping the pot with his right. Obviously, this made it very difficult to make the pot symmetrical and its surface smooth. An improvement in technique came in the New Kingdom: An assistant turned the wheel, allowing the potter to work the clay with both hands. A slightly better wheel was introduced in the late New Kingdom. A potter now spun it with his feet, which eliminated the need for a second person. This was not the true potter's wheel—the "kick wheel," operated by a pedal—however, which the Greeks introduced into Egypt during the Ptolemaic Period.

The third and fourth steps in making coarse ware were drying and firing, or baking. After leaving his pots out in the sun to

Ceramics in the Old Kingdom

In this excerpt from her book about life during Egypt's Old Kingdom, scholar Jill Kamil outlines some of the basic methods of potters in that era.

Several different techniques were employed. Most vessels were hand-formed entirely . . . and use was also made of the hand-wheel [which the potter turned with one hand]. Pottery was left to dry in the open air to what is usually called the "leather-hard stage." It was then smoothed by the potter's hand, or with a cloth, after which a coating of pigment and water, or pigment mixed with clay and water, could be added to the surface before the pottery was fired. These coatings made the surface less permeable [porous], and improved the appearance of the vessel.

This vase showing a ship dates from shortly before the Old Kingdom.

dry thoroughly, the potter prepared his firing materials. For many centuries the baking process was, like the shaping stage, primitive because of the low level of available technology. Firing took place in open bonfires fueled by wood and animal dung. Eventually, potters developed cylindrical firing ovens, or kilns, which, though they used the same fuel as the bonfires, better contained the heat. "Near the base of each oven," which was as tall as a person, Eugen Strouhal writes,

> was a small opening for fuel . . . to be put in and stoked from time to time. Above the fire-chamber was a large upper opening through which the work could be stacked on a perforated clay grid. A wooden block, sometimes with steps, enabled the potter to reach this level. During firing, the upper opening was covered except for a small gap to let the smoke out. Modern analysis of vessels made in this way shows that the ovens must have developed temperatures of 600°–800° C. As soon as the firing-time was up, the potter moved the stepping block close to the lower hole, so as to bank the fire down by cutting off the air supply. Later, he opened the kiln and passed the finished vessels to his mate, who carried them off on a yoke.[13]

Ptolemaic Pottery

In Ptolemaic times, potters used the methods that Greek potters had developed over many centuries. In large part, these were the same techniques the Egyptian potters had employed. However, the Greeks' technology was more sophisticated, which allowed for production of higher-quality wares in greater numbers. The pedal-driven kick wheel turned out pots much faster than earlier Egyptian wheels, for instance; this stimulated true mass production of pottery, much of which was exported to other lands.

Pottery in the Ptolemaic Period was also distinctive because much of it was decorated with finely painted figures and scenes, a long-standing tradition of Greek ceramics. The two most popular Ptolemaic styles of pottery were black-glazed and Hadra. Cups, bowls, vases, and other vessels in the black-glazed style were ribbed and featured black floral designs on a white background. Of the Hadra pots, some featured decorative panels applied in black on a pale brown background. Others had multicolored images of shields, swords, and other objects painted on a white background.

In addition to native-made pottery, Ptolemaic cities, especially the capital, Alexandria (on the Mediterranean coast in the western Nile Delta), imported foreign varieties. A wide range of ceramics were imported from Greece, Italy, Asia Minor, and other areas. The majority of these imported vessels were too pricey for average Egyptians, most of whom continued to use cheaper native ceramics.

Production of Faience

Meanwhile, members of the upper classes bought not only imported clay pottery but also locally made faience products. Fine

An array of finely decorated faience objects from the Eighteenth Dynasty includes two bowls, a bracelet, and a jewelry box.

lamps, bowls, vases, statuettes, and other kinds of Egyptian faience that featured a characteristic apple-green glaze were made in Alexandria in Ptolemaic times. Demand for vessels made of faience was nothing new, however, as these items had been very popular in Egypt for nearly three millennia. (The first examples had appeared in the Early Dynastic Period.)

The Egyptian word for faience was *tjehenet*, meaning "dazzling." This referred to the shiny, at times iridescent, surface of objects made of this material. Indeed, the beauty of faience objects, as opposed to the drabness of coarse ware, made faience a colorful, cheaper substitute for semiprecious stones such as lapis lazuli, turquoise, and malachite.

Most Egyptian faience was made of crushed quartz, a hard, translucent variety of stone. After crushing the quartz using stone pounding balls, the artisan mixed the powder with water and small amounts of lime and/or plant ash to produce a paste. He then shaped the paste into the desired objects. These included beads, amulets (objects thought to possess magical powers), and decorative tiles, as well as figurines, vases, and other items also widely made as coarse ware.

After shaping an object, the faience potter applied the all-important glaze, also in the form of a paste. Most of the glazes were bluish or greenish in hue, although other colors were employed as well. The color depended on the ingredients in the glaze paste, as Rosalie David explains:

> The usual colors of blue, green, or greenish-blue were achieved by adding compounds of copper to the glaze, which was either a sodium-calcium silicate or a potassium-calcium silicate [minerals fairly prevalent in Egypt]. Other colors, such as violet, white, yellow, red, and black, were produced by adding different ingredients. Green and blue faience were nonetheless the most popular colors because they most

closely imitated the . . . [very popular] semi-precious stones malachite and lapis lazuli.[14]

After adding the glaze, the potter fired the object, which caused the glaze to harden and strongly adhere to the quartz-paste core. Sometimes the artisan performed an additional step and added decoration to the piece. He might paint on designs in black paint or add details using a different colored faience paste, after which he baked the pot a second time.

Early Egyptian Glassmaking

Egyptian glassware was related to Egyptian faience because both were made from crushed quartz or sand. The major difference between the two craft disciplines was that faience was mostly opaque, whereas glass was transparent, or nearly so. Small

A stone relief depicts glassblowers at work. Glassmaking reached high levels of quality in the New Kingdom, the Ptolemaic Period, and Roman times.

amounts of glass were first produced in Egypt during the Middle Kingdom. But glassmaking did not become an important local industry until the Eighteenth Dynasty, in the first centuries of the New Kingdom. Even then, the art was tightly controlled by the royal court, which had imported glassmaking techniques from Syria during Egyptian military expeditions into the Near East. For instance, the first known major Egyptian glassmaking workshop was erected near the royal palace during the reign of the pharaoh Amenhotep III (ca. 1390–1352 B.C.). For a long time, therefore, only royal and wealthy Egyptians had access to glass products.

The basic technique used in such New Kingdom workshops was what is sometimes called the core-forming method. First, sand was melted at high temperatures until it turned into molten (liquid) glass. The artisan had already prepared cores of the vessels he wanted to make, each core essentially a molded piece of ordinary coarse ware. With the aid of a metal handling rod, the artisan dipped the cores into the molten glass, a layer of which adhered to each core. Then he allowed the objects to cool, a process known as annealing. When cooling and hardening were complete, the glassmaker jabbed pointed instruments through the opening in each vessel to break up and remove the core material, leaving the glass shell intact.

Another technique called cold cutting was employed less often because it was very difficult and required great skill. The artisan made molten glass in the usual way and allowed it to cool somewhat until it became a malleable mass. Then he cut off lumps of the material, carefully molded them into the shapes desired, and allowed them to cool. Two exquisite glass headrests found in the tomb of the pharaoh Tutankhamun (better known today as King Tut, who reigned ca. 1336–1327 B.C.) were made using this method.

A third early glassmaking technique was molding, in which the molten glass was poured into wooden molds. "At its simplest," in Ian Shaw's words,

this involved the making of plain glass forms, but it could also be much more complex, with sections of glass cane [rods or elongated lumps] of different colors fused together in a mold to make multicolored vessels, such as those with yellow eyes [beads] on a green background.[15]

Glassmaking in Ptolemaic and Roman Egypt

Partly because glassmaking was so closely tied to the royal court, the industry rapidly declined in the second half of the New Kingdom, when the pharaohs became increasingly weak. By the end of the era the country was wracked by political dissension and economic troubles. The glassmaking shops suffered as a result and disappeared altogether by the start of the Third Intermediate Period (ca. 1069–747 B.C.).

A revival of glassmaking occurred in the fourth century B.C., in early Ptolemaic times. In the thriving economy maintained

Chapter Three

CLOTH MAKING AND LEATHER WORKING

A rchaeological evidence shows that cloth making and leather working were among the oldest crafts practiced in Egypt. Cloth making developed at least as early as the first half of Neolithic times, and some form of leather working was likely widespread in the Nile Valley tens of thousands of years earlier still. In large part, this was because these were the basic clothes-making crafts. And people in societies worldwide began wearing some form of clothing in the Stone Age.

Leather was made from animal hides, the first known clothing material. Later, the Egyptians learned to harvest and exploit flax, a highly versatile plant. From the seeds they obtained linseed oil, and from the stems they took fibers that they transformed into linen, the country's most common textile throughout its long history. Leather remained in use for sandals and shoes but was only occasionally used for loincloths and other clothing items; it was also used widely for rope, pouches, tents, and other nonclothing items.

The Egyptians learned to make textiles from other materials as well, including sheep's wool, cotton, and silk. But for various reasons these were never as important as linen. Wool, for instance, was less useful because it is a relatively heavy and warm fabric, not as suitable in Egypt's warm, mild climate as lighter, cooler linen. A few simple, lightweight linen garments were developed early (especially among the lower classes, which made up the bulk of the population) and remained in use for the rest of antiquity. "Although most men of the lower classes wore a simple loincloth," Rosalie David points out,

kings and the wealthy are usually shown [in wall paintings and sculptures] in kilts. The details of these varied to some extent, but the garment remained the same from the Old Kingdom to the Roman Period [30 B.C.–A.D. 395]. The upper classes sometimes added a tunic, shirt, or cloak. Women

At left, an Egyptian uses a sickle to harvest flax; below are surviving examples of Egyptian linen.

of the nobility and upper classes are shown in narrow dresses held under the bosom by two wide straps suspended from the shoulders. From the New Kingdom [on] they sometimes also added a cloak.[16]

Making the cloth for these and other garments involved two general craft processes: spinning and weaving. In spinning, a person creates thread by pulling fibers from plant stems or animal hair and twisting them until they are of a desired thickness and strength. Weaving is the process in which the threads are intertwined—either by hand or by a mechanical loom—to form cloth.

The Cloth Makers: Women vs. Men

In Egypt, both of these processes were at first practiced almost exclusively by women, so that cloth making was one of the few ancient crafts in which women predominated, at least during some eras. (Although spinning, weaving, and clothes making were long done by women in Egypt, laundering the clothes was always done by men.) Moreover, for dozens of centuries—throughout Neolithic and Predynastic times—this work was a cottage industry, with the women of each family or village making the fabrics and clothing for their relatives and neighbors. No formal textile workshops, in which people produced cloth on a bigger scale for larger groups, existed until the Old Kingdom.

At first, the women in such workshops did not serve the general public and open markets, as a majority of Egyptians continued to make their clothes in their own homes. For a long time, these shops turned out fabrics and clothing mainly for the royal palace and upper classes. It is possible that some of the shops were run and staffed by members of the pharaohs' harems (groups of royal wives).

Evidence for a royal linen workshop was found in a princess's tomb dating from the Fifth Dynasty (ca. 2494–2345 B.C.). An inscription reads, "Khenemu, subject of the king . . . assistant, superintendent of the weaving workshop."[17] Though short, the inscription is very informative. First, it connects the king to the shop, suggesting that it produced cloth for the palace. In addition, it provides the name of an individual craftsman, a rarity in ancient records. Since Khenemu was a woman, the inscription also shows that women were allowed to manage fabric-making shops, at least in the Old Kingdom.

Over time, however, this situation changed. In the Middle Kingdom male supervisors became increasingly common in the cloth workshops. And from the New Kingdom on, more and more male work-

A model found in an Eleventh-Dynasty tomb depicts a group of women weaving cloth in a workshop.

ers staffed the shops until by Roman times men predominated in the industry (though a few women remained). The reasons for this major shift in gender are unknown.

Materials for Fabric

Whether women or men spun and wove the cloth, they used the same sources and raw materials. Egyptian farmers began to grow flax, the main source of fibers for fabric, in the Neolithic Age. The flax stems were harvested by hand and then pulled through a wooden device that looked something like a big comb in order to remove leaves and other extraneous materials. The stems consisted partially of hard, tough fibers and softer, more pliable fibers. To separate the softer fibers, which would be used to make cloth, from the harder ones, the workers soaked the stems in water and then beat them with wooden mallets. The separated fibers were then ready to be spun into thread to make linen.

Although sheep's wool was used much less often than flax linen in ancient Egypt, some people did wear woolen cloaks over their tunics from time to time, mainly on unseasonably cold nights. Also, in Roman times it became customary to weave colored woolen threads into linen fabrics as an added decoration. In addition, wool was used in making wigs, which were worn by both men and women.

The Egyptian attitude toward wool changed over time, partly because of changing religious beliefs. In pharaonic Egypt, in which many gods were worshipped, wool was not allowed in temples or tombs because it was viewed as ritually unclean (a fact re-

Pliny Describes the Cotton Tree

Cotton was somewhat rare in Egypt until the Roman Period. As late as the first century A.D., the Roman scholar Pliny the Elder described the fiber as an oddity native to certain Eastern lands (in this case Persia). The excerpt is from his Natural History.

Also in the Persian Gulf is the island of Tyros. . . . On the island's higher ground there are trees that bear "wool," but in a different way from those of the Chinese, for the leaves of these trees have no such "wool," and, were they not smaller, might be thought to be vine-leaves. The trees bear gourds [small round pods]. . . . When these ripen and open up, they reveal balls of "down" from which an expensive linen material for clothes is made. Local people call this the "cotton tree." It also grows, more profusely, on the smaller island of Tyros, which is 10 miles from the other island of the same name. . . . The linen produced from this is of a higher quality than its Indian counterpart.

ported by Herodotus soon after his trip to Egypt). In contrast, the monotheistic Christians had no such taboos regarding wool or other fabrics. After Christianity became widespread in Egypt in late Roman times, placing woolen garments in graves and tombs became commonplace.

A wall painting from the Middle Kingdom shows workers spinning yarn. Egyptian yarn was typically made from fibers of flax or wool.

Other kinds of animal hair were occasionally used to weave cloaks but were more often employed in making carrying bags. These included goat's hair and camel's hair, which, like sheep's wool, was periodically sheared (cut) off the animals and cleaned or otherwise treated before spinning it into yarn.

Cotton arrived in Egypt fairly late in the country's agricultural history. Originally grown in India on small trees up to ten feet tall, cotton made its way to Egypt through Eastern trade routes. The first Egyptian cotton garments were probably made in the sixth century B.C. (during the Late Period, ca. 747–332). Widespread manufacture of cotton cloth did not begin until the Roman Period, however. The first-century-A.D. Roman scholar Pliny the Elder said that cotton trees became common in southern Egypt, Nubia (the land directly south of Egypt proper), and the nearby Red Sea island of Tyl. Cotton trees produce small wads of tiny fibers that grow around each seed. The ancients, including the Egyptians, removed the fibers from the seeds (by hand or with a comb) to prepare it for spinning.

Another late arrival, silk (which comes from very thin fibers made by silkworms), originated in China. Fully formed silk cloth, which like cotton moved westward along the trade routes, appeared in Egypt in the Ptolemaic Period. But not until the sixth century A.D., after the close of the Roman Period, did the production of silk begin in Egypt.

Spinning and Weaving

Whether the fibers came from flax, wool, cotton, or silk, they had to be spun into thread (or yarn) for weaving. Throughout most of Egypt's history the spinning process was accomplished either by hand (by twisting the raw fibers with the fingers) or by using spindles.

A typical spindle was a wooden or bone rod about six to nine inches long that was a bit thicker toward the lower end. The spinner used his or her fingers to twist a thread out of a mass of fibers and attach the thread to the spindle. Sometimes with the aid of a small attached weight called a whorl, the spindle spun; as the spinner pulled more loosely connected fibers from the mass, the rotating spindle twisted them into threads. (The distaff, a forked stick that held the mass of fibers, was not introduced into Egypt until the Roman Period.)

The spun thread was woven on looms. These were fairly primitive, particularly the horizontal variety in use up until the end of the Middle Kingdom. Essentially they consisted of a rectangular frame of four narrow poles resting on pegs set in the ground. The weavers stretched rows of thread (collectively called the warp) across the frame from one side to the opposite side. Then, often working in pairs, they interwove another set of threads (the weft) at a right angle into the warp. One common method was to connect the end of the weft thread to a stick called the shuttle. One weaver worked the shuttle under and over the warp threads. At a certain point, the weaver tossed the shuttle to another weaver sitting or squatting on the far side of the loom, who interwove a new weft row back in the first weaver's direction. In this way the shuttle passed back and forth and the threads formed a piece of fabric.

A slightly more advanced loom appeared shortly before the beginning of the New Kingdom. It also had a rectangular wooden frame, only in this case the frame stood in a vertical position and the weavers interwove the threads from the bottom up. The warp threads hung vertically from the top bar of the loom. These were weighted by small rocks or lumps of baked clay. The weaver sat in front of the loom and passed horizontal weft threads in and out of the warp with the aid of a comb or stick. The linen cloth made on such looms was often of very high quality. Thread counts of 160 (warp) by 120 (weft) per inch, comparable to many modern fabrics, were common.

Laundering Cloth

Like cloth in every time and place, that produced by ancient Egyptian workers had to be laundered from time to time. Generally this was done in rivers by scrubbing the cloth with natron (a mineral salt) and then rinsing it thoroughly. In her book about village life in Egypt, scholar A.G. McDowell includes the following translations of two fragmented documents recording laundry lists.

1. Work given to the washerman Baki:
   House of [?]: kilts, 2; underpants, 2; tunics [?]; sleeve, 1; [head]bands, 3. House of Khonsu: kilt, 1; loincloth, 1; shawl, 1; underpants, 1; sleeve, 1; rags [?].

2. Year 1, third month of winter, day 15. This day, giving clothes to the washerman. . . . Given to him at the riverbank to launder: 10 kilts, 8 loincloths, 5 sanitary towels.

Leather Products and Workers

High-quality products were also turned out by Egyptian leather workers. Most leather was made from the hides of cattle, goats, oxen, gazelles, and donkeys, but the skins of other animals were used as well. Animal coats considered exceptionally beautiful, such as those of leopards and certain kinds of antelope, were not stripped of their fur to make leather; instead, the fur-covered skins became decorative covers for chairs and shields or special clothing items for the wealthy. Typical leather products included quivers for arrows, carrying bags, tents, mattresses for beds, wall hangings, bracelets, dog collars, straps and thongs used in making various weapons, and sandals and shoes.

A fair amount is known about leather making in Egypt thanks to some surviving tomb paintings depicting the leather workers (known as *tjebu*) in various stages of their craft. The most comprehensive example was found in a tomb near ancient Thebes that belonged to Rekhmire, vizier (chief administrator) under the early New Kingdom pharaohs Thutmose III (reigned ca. 1479–1425 B.C.) and Amenhotep II (ca. 1427–1400 B.C.). Eugen Strouhal describes the leather workers in the painted scene:

> One is stretching out the roughly cut pieces of leather, others are tracing the outlines of sandals, others again are making holes round the sole-edges with an awl [a pointed tool] or horn, another is cutting out straps which the last of the team is threading through the holes. One of them, having to use both hands to grip the sole, is tugging at the projecting end of a strap with his teeth. . . . Other leather products are shown in their finished state, such as pouches, sacks, bellows, parchment rolls, and jackets.[18]

Making Leather and Leather Products

Each of the workers shown in the painting was a specialist in some aspect of the leather-making profession. There were three major stages of leather working, the first of which was processing the hides. This involved removing the fur or hair from the hide and scraping away the fatty tissue lying directly beneath it.

The next stage was curing, or treating, the hide to preserve it from rotting and convert it into workable leather. Various curing methods were employed, including subjecting the hides to smoke from a fire, rubbing them with salt, or dipping them in vats of sesame oil. True tanning, which uses tannin (or tannic acid) as a curing agent, was also practiced. Most common of all the curing methods employed in ancient Egypt, however, was tawing. This consisted of rubbing the hides thoroughly with alum (potassium aluminum sulfate), a mineral found in a handful of desert oases. After curing, the tanners softened the leather by treating it with fat or animal (or human) urine or dung and then stretched it. These steps were necessary because alum and other curing agents could make the leather stiff.

Leather workers make shoe soles, laces, and buckles in a section of a detailed painting from the New Kingdom tomb of the vizier Rekhmire.

Sometimes dyeing the leather was part of the curing process. The most popular color was red, which was produced by a dye made from the roots of the madder, a plant that grows wild in southern Asia, or from ground-up specimens of a Mediterranean insect called the cochineal bug. Pomegranate juice was used to produce a yellow dye. The source of a popular green dye has not yet been identified.

The last stage of leather making consisted of cutting the leather into the desired shapes and fashioning the pieces into various goods. Leather ropes or straps were often used to hold together such goods. For example, holes punched in the top of a leather carrying bag could be threaded with a long leather strap, the ends of which could be tied to shut the top of the bag.

A similar method used leather thongs to hold the soles of leather sandals on one's feet. Sandal making and shoe making were among the most common and important craft industries that utilized leather in ancient Egypt. Painted scenes of shoemakers hard at work have been found in several tombs, including that of the vizier Rekhmire. According to David:

The shoemaker put the prepared leather on his sloping worktable and cut it into soles or straps, using a knife with a curved blade and a short handle. Then, using a piercer [made of a

A pair of sandals from the Predynastic Period illustrates how the leather thongs were knotted in three places.

sharpened piece of bone or copper] he made holes in the skin through which the thongs would be drawn. The workman pulled these through with his teeth and fastened them with knots, thus producing the simplest form of sandal.[19]

Cloth making and leather working are excellent examples of the merger of artistic craftsmanship and practicality in ancient Egypt. These and many other crafts were first and foremost concerned with turning out products for practical use. Yet the craftsmen were mostly skilled artisans who took pride in their workmanship. Though a shop might produce items in quantity, each was handmade and unique and, more often than not, of very high quality.

Chapter Four

WORKING WITH METAL AND WOOD

Compared to the very ancient skills of fashioning stone tools and vessels, making pottery, cloth making, and leather working, large-scale production of metal and wood items appeared relatively late in ancient Egypt. The metalworking and woodworking crafts did not become prominent until the late Predynastic Period. For the remainder of antiquity, however, they remained among the country's most crucial craft industries.

As was the case with other Egyptian craftsmen, metalworkers and woodworkers were usually not viewed as artists in the modern sense of the word. Instead, they were simply skilled workers. As such, they occupied a position on the social ladder only slightly higher than that of ordinary menial laborers. Not only did the true artistic talents of these artisans go largely unrecognized but much of the credit for what they achieved was often usurped by the upper-class people they worked for. For example, above a painted panel of woodworkers plying their trade in the vizier Rekhmire's tomb appears the following inscription: "Making furniture in ivory and ebony . . . in real cedar from the heights of the terraced hills, by this official who establishes guide-lines and controls the hands of his craftsmen."[20] As scholar T.G.H. James points out:

Rekhmire is thus made out to be the source and inspiration of the skills of the craftsmen under his control—part of the general fiction which allowed the great, from the king downwards, to claim for themselves all the credit in the achievements more properly belonging to their subordinates.[21]

The Difficulties of Copper Mining

Although they credit the artisans, and not upper-class officials, with considerable skill, modern scholars and other observers also point out the shortcomings of the artisans' work. For example, after close study of the development of Egyptian metalworking, the general consensus is that, with the possible exception of gold working, this was less advanced and sophisticated in ancient Egypt than it was in several neighboring western Asian and eastern Mediterranean areas.

One reason for this was that Egypt possessed few natural deposits of metals. For the most part, therefore, the metals had to be mined in or imported from faraway places, which was difficult and expensive. Second, Egypt had few forests; this meant that it lacked much of the wood needed to fuel the fires in which metal was smelted. Finally, the tradition-oriented Egyptians continued to use stone tools and weapons longer and in larger numbers than neighboring peoples, who switched to metal earlier. The Egyptian switch to metal was gradual and conservative, following metalworking methods developed long before by others.

Despite these impediments, a thriving metal industry did eventually develop in Egypt and some metalsmiths (called *bedjty*, after the name for metal vases) became highly skilled. The main metals worked were copper, gold, silver, iron, tin, and lead. And the four principal alloys (mixtures of two or more metals) were bronze (copper and tin), electrum (gold and silver), brass (copper and zinc), and a mixture of copper and lead.

Copper was the first metal the Egyptians exploited. Some copper smelting occurred in the late Predynastic Period, but not until the Third and Fourth dynasties (ca. 2686–2494, B.C.) had copper tools and weapons largely replaced stone ones. For a long time the main source of copper was the Sinai Peninsula, on the eastern coast of the Red Sea. (Later, the Mediterranean island of Cyprus became an important source.) Thus, to collect the copper ore (rocks containing copper) required a long trip over hot desert sands and rocky terrain. About the year 1830 B.C., a royal official composed this description of the difficult journey:

This land [Sinai] was reached in the third month of the second season.... This [official] says to the officials who may come to this mining area at this season: Let not your faces flag [i.e., expressions become glum] because of it. ... I came from Egypt with my face flagging. It was difficult ... when the land was burning hot ... and the mountains branded a blistered skin.[22]

In the Sinai, at first laborers simply picked up pieces of copper ore off the ground or cut them from surface rocks. But the demand for copper soon made mining necessary. The miners were not craftsmen but menial laborers who toiled for long hours each day under horrendous working conditions. It is somewhat unclear exactly who the early miners were, although a surviving Middle Kingdom document mentions that at least some were slaves. Over time, the vast majority were indeed slaves, mostly convicted criminals and war prisoners. In the second century B.C. (during Ptolemaic times), a Greek geographer named Agatharchides described such workers and their plight:

Nightmare in the Mines

The extreme difficulties of mining metal ores in ancient Egypt (and neighboring lands) were captured graphically in the second century B.C. by a Greek geographer named Agatharchides (translated in Karl Muller's Geographi Graeci Minores*).*

Like these construction workers, miners had to perform backbreaking labor.

The worst of fates falls to those whom the . . . government sends off to the bitter slavery of the . . . mines, some to suffer along with their wives and children. . . . The rock of the mountains in which the gold is found is sheer and very hard. They burn wood fires and render it spongy with heat, and then go at working it, cutting the parts softened up with quarrying tools. . . . Those who are young and strong quarry the gleaming stone with iron picks, delivering their blows not with any particular skill but just force. . . . They do their quarrying with [small oil] lamps bound to their foreheads, following the white gleam like a vein. Constantly shifting the position of their bodies, they knock down chunks—not according to their bodily condition and strength, but to the foreman's eye, who never fails to administer punishment with the whip. Young boys, creeping through the galleries hacked out by the miners, laboriously collect what has fallen down on the gallery floor and carry it outside the entrance. From them the rock is taken over by the more elderly and many of the feeble, who bring it to the so-called choppers. . . . They pound the rock vigorously with iron pestles until they have made the biggest piece the size of a pea.

The worst of fates falls to those whom the . . . government sends off to the bitter slavery of the . . . mines, some to suffer along with their wives and children. . . . The rock of the mountains in which the [metal] is found is sheer and very hard. . . . They do their quarrying with [small oil] lamps bound to their foreheads. . . . Constantly shifting the position of their bodies, they knock down chunks—not according to their bodily condition and strength, but to the foreman's eye, who never fails to administer punishment with the whip. Young boys . . . laboriously collect what has fallen down on the gallery floor and carry it outside the entrance. From them the rock is taken over by the more elderly and many of the feeble, who . . . pound the rock vigorously with iron pestles until they have made the biggest piece the size of a pea. . . . All who suffer the fate just described feel that death is more desirable than life.[23]

Smelting and Casting

Once the ore was mined, the precious metal had to be separated from the rocky parts of the ore. The smelting process involved placing the ore in a stone container and heating it over an open fire. A standard fire did not produce high enough temperatures to melt the ore, so smelters had to find ways to raise the temperature by increasing the fire's oxygen supply. At first this was done by having several people (often boys, perhaps apprentices) blow through hollow reeds. In the New Kingdom, however, a rudimentary form of bellows was introduced. According to Strouhal:

This consisted of a shallow earthenware [pottery] dish covered in leather [usually goatskin], out of which an air tube was directed toward the fire. A single worker could operate two pairs of bellows alternately, pressing one down with his foot and raising the other with a string. This device produced a higher temperature than the blow-pipes, increased productivity, and reduced the effort required.[24]

The next step was to cast the separated copper (or other metal) into the desired shape. The earliest and simplest method consisted of beating, cutting, and bending the metal. First, workers used long, sturdy sticks to pick up the hot container holding the liquid metal. Carefully, they poured the metal onto a wide stone slab or into a deeper stone dish. After allowing the metal to cool somewhat and partially solidify, they used oval stones or stone hammers (later metal hammers) to beat the metal mass into shape. At various stages in the solidifying process, they could cut and bend the metal, further shaping it by more beating or by rubbing it with oval stones.

Later, the artisans learned to use more advanced metal-casting techniques that had developed in other lands. One, which used negative molds, was fairly straightforward. They created a mold by chipping it out of a piece of stone and then poured the liquid metal into the mold. After it dried, they removed the solid metal object from the mold.

In a more complex process known as hollow casting, the artisans began by making a wooden model of the object they wanted to create later in metal. They covered the model with clay and fired it. Then they removed the wooden core, leaving a hollow pottery mold. Finally, they poured liquid metal into the mold. Once it solidified they removed the pottery, leaving the desired metal object.

In the New Kingdom still another casting technique, the *ciré perdue*, or "lost wax," method, was introduced for delicate, highly detailed items such as figurines. "A beeswax model of the object to be produced was coated with clay to form the mold," Rosalie David explains.

This was then imbedded in sand or earth, which formed a support, and was heated so that the beeswax melted and ran out of the holes in the mold. Hardened and rigid, the mold was then ready to receive the molten metal, which was poured in through the holes. Once this had cooled down, the mold was broken and the metal object was released.[25]

Bronze, Gold, and Other Metals

These same smelting and casting techniques were used for other metals besides copper, with some small variations depending on the kind of metal and types of objects being made. Bronze appeared during the Middle Kingdom, at first mainly as an import from Syria. But it was not produced on a

Goldsmiths pour molten gold into molds in this detail from a tomb painting. After the metal solidified, the workers removed it from the molds.

large scale and did not largely replace copper until the New Kingdom. (Even then, copper and stone items continued to supplement bronze ones.) Tin, when added in proportions of 3 to 16 percent to copper, gave bronze its extra hardness. The main source of the tin was Mesopotamia. Camel and mule caravans carried the scarce tin from the hills southeast of Babylon to Syria, from which ships carried it to Egypt and other lands.

Gold and silver were other scarce metals prized by the Egyptians. They got their gold in large part from the deserts lying between the Nile River and Red Sea, although some came from farther south in Nubia and from other foreign locales. Because gold was so rare and highly valued, it was not usually cast into solid objects. (Exceptions were golden masks and coffins cast for some of the pharaohs, including those found in King Tut's tomb.) Instead, most gold was either beaten into very thin sheets to become gold leaf or (while still in liquid form) plated onto bronze objects such as bracelets, scepters, expensive dinnerware, and ceremonial swords. Silver (and its alloy, electrum) was handled similarly. Because no silver deposits existed in Egypt and this metal always had to be imported, for several centuries it was even more highly valued than gold.

Although gold working of some kind was known in Egypt early in its history, iron smelting came to Egypt very late. The Egyptians knew about iron from at least as early as the Predynastic Period. But except for a few meteorites and some rare, tiny deposits, they had no native supplies of this hard, tough metal. Some iron weapons and other iron objects began to be imported during the New Kingdom. But the first significant iron smelting did not begin in Egypt until Greek colonists living in Naukratis (in the western Nile Delta) introduced it in the sixth century B.C. And the industry did not become widespread and important until Roman times.

Carpentry Materials and Tools

Like metal smelting, large-scale woodworking developed fairly late in Egypt. Carpenters and other woodworkers did not emerge as major craftsmen until the late Predynastic Period, not long before the first pharaohs began to rule. There were two main reasons for this. First, Egypt lacked forests and its few usable native woods—acacia, tamarisk, date palm, and willow—were in scarce supply. In late Predynastic and Early Dynastic times, increased foreign trade introduced a wider range of trees, including cedar, cypress, elm, juniper, maple, oak, and pine, thus making more wood available.

Second, the Egyptians had begun to fashion copper tools. Some of these, including axes, chisels, saws, awls, drills (worked by hand or by bows), and nails, made working with wood easier, faster, and more exact, thereby making it possible to create high-quality furniture and other wooden products. (The copper carpentry tools were eventually replaced by bronze versions.)

One of the most useful of the new tools was the bow-operated drill. It consisted of

King Tut's Gold

Some of the finest examples of the art of Egyptian goldsmiths were uncovered in the tomb of the pharaoh Tutankhamun ("King Tut") in 1922. Often, the gold work was combined with the art of the country's best woodworkers. The most impressive examples are a series of three coffins, one nestled within another. The outer two coffins are carved from wood and gilded with gold leaf (made by pounding thin sheets of gold with mallets). The innermost coffin, which held the boy king's mummy, is made of pure gold and weighs almost three hundred pounds. There were also thirty wooden statues in the tomb, each plated in gold. Some show Tut himself hunting; others depict various Egyptian gods or protective spirits. In addition, the tomb contained numerous pieces of finely made gold jewelry, including necklaces, pectorals, and earrings. Finally, the excavators found several gold-covered wooden crooks and flails (symbols of Egyptian royalty), including the pair the pharaoh held on the day of his coronation.

Several gold-coated objects are visible in this museum reconstruction of part of King Tut's tomb.

a wooden wand or cylinder with a metal tip attached to one end. The operator held the drill upright between the curved wooden handle and string of a small bow (held at a right angle to the wand). He ran the string back and forth along the vertical wand, turning it so that the metal point at the tip of the wand twisted slowly but steadily into the wood.

Another somewhat revolutionary carpentry tool was the saw. Egyptian saws were "pull" saws, having the cutting edge of their teeth set toward the handle. (By contrast, most modern saws are "push" saws whose teeth are set away from the handle.) Metal saws not only greatly re-

duced the time it took to cut through wooden planks but also produced smoother, more even cuts.

Common Wooden Items

With the ready availability of a wide range of wood types and the proper tools, woodworking fast became an art, one of the most outstanding in the country's history. Carpenters learned to use specific kinds of wood for specific items to achieve the best possible results. Sycamore and cedar were often preferred for large objects that required thick planks, such as tables, doors, chests, coffins, and big statues. Very hard

Two carpenters employ a bow-drill in a detail from the painting in Rekhmire's tomb. The man above them uses a saw to cut a board.

Middle sections of the painting from the tomb of Rekhmire show wood-carvers and carpenters at work. Among the tools depicted are saws and chisels.

woods such as tamarisk were employed for making wooden mallets and tool handles, and acacia was a favorite choice for the decks and masts of boats. Chairs, stools, small boxes, figurines, and many other small objects were made from maple, oak, pine, and other imported woods.

Egyptian carpenters were particularly adept at making furniture. A number of well-preserved examples of such furniture have survived, mostly in a handful of unplundered tombs discovered in the twenti-eth century. King Tut's tomb, found in 1922, for example, yielded 6 chairs, 12 stools, 6 beds, and 69 storage chests and boxes, most in good condition and many decorated with inlays of ivory, ebony, or other exotic materials. One of the chairs is a magnificent thronelike seat decorated in gold. (In accordance with religious custom, these items were intended for Tut's use in the afterlife.)

More finely decorated wooden furniture was discovered in 1906 in the tomb of an overseer named Kha, who died in the

The thronelike seat from King Tut's tomb demonstrates finely detailed inlays of gold, faience, glass, and various semiprecious stones.

fourteenth century B.C. Among these pieces are nine stools, the most common sitting devices in ancient Egypt. The most elaborate of the nine "is of a folding construction," says James.

Its supports end in duck heads inlaid with ivory, grasping in their beaks the cross-bars which provide stability to the piece. This stool . . . is made of hard wood imported from tropical Africa—a choice piece that shows no signs of having been made specially for the tomb [suggesting that such fine craftsmanship was a common feature of everyday furniture].[26]

It was also common to inlay portions of wooden chairs, storage boxes, and coffins with faience, colored stones, or glass. In this way, two or more of Egypt's craft disciplines combined to produce practical items that were as well made and beautiful as the finest examples made today.

Chapter Five

Jewelry Making and Painting

Two crafts at which the ancient Egyptians excelled, producing artistic works rich in vibrant colors, were jewelry making and painting. Rudimentary forms of both disciplines existed as early as Neolithic times in the Nile Valley. Scenes depicting hunting, herds of animals, and small riverboats were drawn on cliffs in southern Egypt and Nubia in the 7000s B.C. And in the two millennia that followed, people were buried wearing necklaces, bracelets, amulets of shell and ivory, and belts made of green beads.

Over time, jewelry makers and painters honed their crafts. By the advent of the Old Kingdom, the Egyptians were producing very fine examples of jewelry made of gold and precious gems, as well as beautifully executed wall paintings in tombs and temples. Painting remained one of the premier crafts in Egypt for some three thousand years. Jewelry making also remained an important craft, although modern experts agree that the finest quality jewelry was produced during the Middle Kingdom.

Beauty and Status Symbols

One obvious reason for the rise of jewelry making was that the early Egyptians admired bright, shiny, colorful objects; and the most common items incorporated into jewelry—gold, silver, gems, ivory, copper, polished colored stones, faience, and glass—fulfilled these criteria. Males and females of all ages wore various kinds of jewelry. Jewelry was also used to adorn the bodies of the dead in tombs and statues of the gods.

Equally obvious to the Egyptians, but less so to most modern observers, was the use of jewelry to denote social and economic status. With occasional exceptions, members of the lower classes wore costume jewelry fashioned from polished stones (such as steatite, obsidian, and alabaster) and faience. So it was easy to pick out people of modest means on the streets or in other public places.

In contrast, people of wealth and high status wore jewelry made of gold, silver, ivory,

Grids to Ensure Proper Proportions

In this excerpt from an essay in David Silverman's Ancient Egypt, *scholar Rita Freed gives a helpful description of the grids used in the canons of proportion employed by painters, sculptors, and other Egyptian craftsmen.*

In a modern reenactment, an ancient painter uses a grid as a guide.

At least as early as the Old Kingdom, the Egyptians perfected a way of replicating their ideal concept of the human image in sculpture and relief. . . . Some of the technical devices used by artisans to achieve symmetry and the desired proportions are still in place [in surviving tombs]. For example, a line runs vertically down a number of servant figures, exactly bisecting their torsos. Horizontal lines intersect the central axis line at the hairline, base of the neck, armpit, elbow, base of the buttocks, and top of the knee. By the Middle Kingdom, these guidelines were fleshed out both horizontally and vertically into a full grid of eighteen squares that extended from the hairline to the bottom of the feet. The grid was further subdivided during the Twenty-sixth Dynasty into twenty-one squares, which allowed even greater control. The Egyptians could lay out these lines on any surface to reproduce identically proportioned figures of whatever size they wanted.

and rare gemstones. Gold was the most popular, partly because of its rarity but also because its sheen was thought to mimic the golden rays emitted by the sun god, Ra, one of Egypt's most important deities. Semiprecious stones, chosen for their color rather than their clarity and refractive qualities (as is the case today), were also popular among the well-to-do. These expensive stones included turquoise, mined in the Sinai; lapis lazuli, imported from Afghanistan; carnelian, found in Egypt's eastern deserts; and amethyst, green feldspar, and garnet. The rich were not reluctant to show off their jewelry; practically any occasion was marked by wearing or giving such finery. According to Rosalie David:

> Kings marked important events in their reigns, such as marriage, accession to the throne, and jubilee festivals, with the production of special sets of jewelry. On some occasions, courtiers presented the king with jewelry to mark a special occasion. Jewelry was also presented [by the pharaohs] to foreign powers and as gifts to favorite courtiers, while certain items were given to mark the appointment of royal officials.[27]

Popular Forms of Jewelry

Whether expensive or cheap, jewelry items followed the same shapes and forms throughout most of the country's history. The most common form was the simple necklace, usually consisting of a single strand of beads, stones, or gems. Cowrie shells, copper beads, and polished stones were popular among the lower classes, gold and gems among the rich.

The well-to-do were also able to afford thicker, more elaborate necklaces called *wesekh*, meaning "broad." Befitting their name,

A tomb painting shows jewelry makers at work. The man at lower left adds beads to a wesekh *collar.*

Egyptian amulets came in a wide variety of shapes and sizes, as seen by these collections from museums.

wesekh were several inches wide and hung in broad bands across the lower neck and upper chest. Another elaborate type of necklace was the pectoral, usually consisting of a rectangular plaque hanging from beaded strands. The plaque contained carved, inlaid, or painted scenes, often of breathtaking detail and beauty. Among the finest surviving examples are pectorals given by the Middle Kingdom pharaoh Amenemhat III to the princess Mereret during the Twelfth Dynasty (ca. 1985–1795 B.C.). Describing one of these artistic masterpieces, Jaromir Malek writes:

The openwork frame is made in the shape of the façade [front] of a small shrine with a decorative cornice [painted or sculpted band] at the top. The name of the king written in a cartouche [oblong outline or shape bearing an inscription] forms the central element and is flanked by other motifs, such as . . . hawk-headed griffins [mythical monsters] trampling fallen enemies. The inlays create a riot of bright red, blue, and green surfaces that

set off the gold silhouettes of the figures and hieroglyphs, yet the openwork [blank spaces between the figures and hieroglyphs], which leaves large spaces free, acts as a restraining force and gives the impression of controlled elegance.[28]

Other common forms of jewelry included armlets, bracelets, anklets, rings, fillets (decorative strands or bands worn in the hair), and earrings. Earrings attained popularity much later than other jewelry forms in Egypt. They did not become common until the advent of the Eighteenth Dynasty, the first royal line of the New Kingdom. And it seems that they were worn mainly by members of the upper classes until much later in the country's history. The most common kind of earring was the hoop. But studs and plugs also became popular in the New Kingdom. "A stud consists of a circular head," James Romano explains,

> either flat or domed, with a projecting shaft. The Egyptians inserted the shaft through a hole in the ear lobe, allowing the round head to rest in the ear. Ear studs made of stone, metal, glass, and faience survive from antiquity. Ear plugs are large disks, each with a deep channel along the edge. They were fitted into holes of enormous proportions punched in the ear lobes.[29]

Amulets were another popular jewelry form. Thought to possess potent magical powers that protected their wearers, amulets were made from a wide range of materials, including polished stones, semiprecious stones, copper, bronze, gold, iron, bone, wood, and faience. Often it was the shape of the amulet that was thought to impart divine protection. A very common example was the ankh (shaped like a cross with a small oval loop at the top), which stood for "life" and supposedly brought the wearer health and longevity. Other popular amulet shapes were the *udjat*, symbolizing the eye of the god Horus, and the scarab, shaped like the beetle of the same name.

Royal Recognition for Painters

Though jewelry makers turned out some of the most popular and widely used products in Egyptian society, like most other craftsmen they were generally viewed more as skilled laborers than as true artists. The only craftsmen in Egypt who came close to attaining the latter status were painters. Beginning in the early years of the Old Kingdom, their work could be found everywhere. They painted pottery vessels; baskets; some jewelry; the walls of houses, temples, palaces, and tombs; coffins; statues; textiles; board games; and more.

Perhaps because the painters' work was so integral to the decoration of royal palaces and tombs, the pharaohs came to prize their craft. An important by-product of this royal appreciation of painting was a significant degree of recognition for the painters themselves. In many cases they received titles indicating high-status and importance. The highest-ranking painters—what later ages would call "masters"—had titles such as "painter of the palace library and sacred books" and "chief painter of the temple of Amun." Also, evidence shows that pharaohs sometimes bestowed gifts on their favorite painters, including cattle and other livestock, land, slaves, or expensive jewelry.

It is not surprising, therefore, that most of the skilled painters worked on royal or upper-class projects or in studios maintained by the wealthy and elite. These craftsmen did not always work in static conditions, however. Many of them likely moved from place to place as dictated by the job and, certainly in the New Kingdom, by the frequent travels of the king and his court. At least some painters were part of the royal residence because they had to be on call to execute their craft whenever the king needed them. When the king traveled, they went with him. As Malek points out:

> From the Eighteenth Dynasty [on] . . . Egypt now had two capitals, at Memphis and Thebes. [The pharaoh] was obliged to stay in different places as state or religious affairs demanded, with the result that there were several royal residencies in various parts of the country. . . . [Each] contained living and ceremonial quarters for the king and his family, [and] buildings housing the palace personnel [including the royal painters]. . . . When the king's presence was required elsewhere, some of his officials and staff probably accompanied him—thus the royal residence moved with the king.[30]

The painters also moved from place to place when their royal patrons lent them out to various courtiers, generals, and other upper-class individuals to work on their homes or tombs.

Pigments and Their Use

Whether they were decorating the king's palace or tomb or some other building or artifact, Egyptian painters, like artists in all eras and places, were dependent on and limited by their tools. Their chief tool was a number of paint pigments derived from readily available natural substances. Their black was derived from soot, for example. And their white came from two pale minerals found in cliffs in various parts of Egypt—chalk and gypsum. To make gray, they mixed black and white.

Other important sources of paint pigments were ochers (varieties of the mineral iron oxide), including red ocher, which produced red pigment; yellow ocher (yellow pigment); and brown ocher (brown pigment). Blue pigment was made by heating a mixture of azurite (a kind of copper ore), natron (a mineral salt), and sand. To get green, they mixed the blue pigment with the yellow pigment obtained from ocher. Mixing red and yellow produced orange, and

Above is a surviving wooden palette and set of reed brushes once used by an Egyptian painter.

Ambitious Middle Kingdom Art

During the Middle Kingdom, Egyptian painters became more ambitious as their subjects expanded in number and often in degree of difficulty. Such subjects included scenes of battles and siege warfare on a larger scale than those seen in the Old Kingdom and depictions of a wide range of sporting events and games. Paintings of wrestling matches became particularly common. Scenes of people interacting with animals were also very prominent in Middle Kingdom art. Some examples show people feeding antelopes, pet baboons helping to harvest figs, and cats lounging in private homes.

Middle Kingdom artisans also attempted to depict movement in space and time in their paintings. They developed a conventional way of showing it by placing identical figures in a sequence, each succeeding figure enacting a part of the action. For example, a young girl's leap into the air was captured in a series of paintings of her—one showing her standing on the ground, a second showing her taking off, a third showing her suspended in midair, and so forth.

Men gather fruit from a fig tree in this Middle Kingdom painting.

combining red and white made pink. In all of these cases, the paint was made by mixing the pigment with water and glue (usually made from the gum of the acacia tree).

Making the paints from the pigments constituted only the first step in the painter's art. He used these colors following conventions (accepted rules and methods) that were handed down from generation to generation, each color or combination of colors symbolizing a specific aspect of nature or the human experience. Light, the dawn, and happiness were evoked using white paint, for instance. By convention, men's skin was rendered in brownish red and women's skin in pale yellow. Bright red often symbolized blood, evil, and violence. And a deeper yellow was used to denote gold, a frequent subject in paintings, especially those on palace and royal tomb walls. Water and turquoise in paintings were depicted in green, a color that also symbolized youth. Blue was used for the sky as well as for the hair of gods (while gods' bodies were usually yellow). Black paint depicted rich soil in painted scenes and also denoted wealth and certain aspects of the afterlife.

Painting Mediums, Methods, and Accessories

These stylistic, almost ritualistic uses of various colored paints were fairly univer-

Even after thousands of years, some of the colors in this painting found in the tomb of the pharaoh Horemheb are still vibrant.

sal among Egyptian painters. A number of specific painting mediums and techniques were likewise common (although slight variations occurred from age to age). Some of these were peculiar to Egypt and differed from those used in neighboring lands.

The Egyptians did not employ the fresco technique (applying the paint to wet plaster), for instance, which was common in many other parts of the Mediterranean world. Instead, they prepared the surface by coating it with various kinds of textured medium and allowing it to dry thoroughly before they began painting. Common mediums included clay mixtures, a paste made from gypsum dust, and white chalk. The chalk, or "gesso," method used a paste created by mixing the powdered chalk with glue (derived from tree gums). The artisans coated a wall, a piece of furniture, a pottery vase, a statue, or even a piece of fabric with the paste, allowed it to dry, and then applied the paint.

The first step in the actual painting process was to sketch outlines of the various parts of the intended scene. This was accomplished by one group of painters known as the draftsmen, or *sesh kedut*. Often they did preliminary sketches on ostraca (pieces of broken pottery), which were abundant in Egypt and a common medium for writing messages and drawing pictures. On a wall or other surface to be painted, the final outlines were usually rendered in red paint and followed the accepted canons of proportion; the canons dictated that arms, legs, and heads would be a certain size in relation to the trunk of a human figure and that various everyday objects would be an acceptable size in the scene. Surviving examples of un-

finished sketches have been found in a number of tombs. In the tomb of the pharaoh Horemheb (reigned ca. 1323–1295 B.C.), for example, a sketch shows a deity holding a staff in one hand and an ankh symbol in the other. The reason that this and some other sketches in the tomb were never completed is unknown.

The finishing work of filling in the sketches with color was performed by another group of painters called simply *sesh*. To apply the paint they used brushes made from the stems of marsh reeds, which grew by the millions in the Nile Delta. An artisan transformed one end of the tool into a brush by chewing on it vigorously and thereby fraying it. Different sized reeds produced different sized brushes, each of which might be chosen for a specialized job. To mix paint, the artisan used a ceramic bowl or conch shell. From these containers, he transferred the paint to a palette. Some palettes were makeshift, such as large ostraca; the painters (or other craftsmen) made more formal and utilitarian ones out of wood or pottery.

When working indoors, especially in tombs, there was little or no natural light. So painters often had to rely on artificial lighting sources. Stone or ceramic lamps that burned oil (derived from various plants) were likely most common, but candles and torches were also employed as lighting accessories. Considering the primitiveness of Egyptian painters' materials, mediums, tools, and accessories, it is truly remarkable that they were able to turn out work of such high quality, surely some of the finest produced in the ancient world.

Chapter Six

WRITING AND LITERATURE

Writing and the creation of literature were not crafts in ancient Egypt in the sense that pottery making, stonemasonry, and painting were. Yet like the traditional crafts, writing and literature required a high degree of skill that only a small segment of the population mastered. Moreover, the Egyptians considered some forms of writing, particularly the picture writing known as hieroglyphics, to be an art form.

One quality of writing that distinguished it from other artistic achievements was that it was widely thought to have magical properties. Many people believed that describing an action in writing made it more likely that the action would occur in real life (by means of magic). A good example was covering the walls of tombs with inscriptions and pictures. During a funeral, someone performed a ritual known as the "opening of the mouth" in the belief that it would, among other things, bring these writings to life after the tomb was sealed.

The special properties of writing and the considerable skills required to become proficient in reading and writing placed these activities well beyond the reach of the vast majority of Egyptians. Most modern scholars estimate that less than 1 percent of the Egyptian population was literate throughout antiquity, although a few suggest the percentage might have been higher in certain eras than in others. A person who managed to master reading and writing was therefore seen as special, and his social status was markedly higher than that of an ordinary craftsman, even a painter. Members of the small, elite group of the literate who devoted their lives to the art of writing were known as scribes (meaning "those who write"). They typically received appointments to high positions in temple priesthoods, the government bureaucracy, and the military, in which they kept records and inventories, composed and answered letters, and created and copied literature.

Writing and literature were defined according to three criteria: the medium, or the material that was written on; the system of symbols, characters, and designs that were the actual writing; and the genre, or subject matter, and purpose of the work. Each of these criteria included several different forms.

Writing Mediums: Stelae and Ostraca

Sometimes a single writing medium was used for several writing purposes. Stelae are a good example. These memorial monuments (usually large slabs of stone engraved with words and pictures), erected by the pharaohs or other high officials, sometimes bore the texts of royal decrees. Others were inscribed with hymns to the gods to celebrate a religious festival.

Quite often stelae commemorated pharaohs' military campaigns and victories. About the year 1294 B.C., for instance, the pharaoh Seti I set up a stela in northern Nubia to commemorate the campaigns in that region by his recently deceased father, Ramesses I. The inscription on the stela first gives the date ("Year 1 [of Seti's reign], fourth month of the third season") and then reads in part:

Lo, his majesty was in the city of Memphis performing the ceremonies of his father. . . . All the gods [of Egypt] . . . gave him [armed] might and victory over all lands, united with one heart under your sandals. . . . His storehouse was filled with male and female slaves from the captivity of [i.e., captured by] his Majesty. . . . [Seti] made a great, august stela of good sandstone [to celebrate his father's achievements].[31]

The "opening of the mouth" ceremony is performed in this vivid painting from the tomb of King Tut.

This modern painting is titled Egyptian Priest Reading a Papyrus. *Scrolls made from papyrus were a common writing medium in Egypt.*

Stelae were very big, formal, and expensive to write on. In contrast, the broken pieces of pottery called ostraca were a small, informal, and very cheap writing medium. Often ostraca bore short and simple personal messages or records of financial transactions of no particular literary merit or importance. But sometimes scribes or others committed true literature to these broken pottery shards. About fifteen hundred literary documents of varying length have been found on ostraca.

The longest of these, the *Tale of Sinuhe,* composed in the early Middle Kingdom, is viewed by many modern experts as the finest masterpiece of ancient Egyptian literature. It tells the story of a young courtier who flees Egypt and has a series of adventures but eventually recognizes the importance of his roots and returns to take part in traditional Egyptian burial and funer-ary rites. In the following excerpt, Sinuhe engages in hand-to-hand combat with a foreign soldier:

A mighty man of Retenu [Syria] came, that he might challenge me in my own camp. He was a hero without peer, and he had [beaten all opponents in his land]. He said that he would fight me, he intended to despoil me, and he planned to plunder my cattle. . . . During the night I strung my bow . . . and I polished my weapons. When day broke, [the men of] Retenu came [to watch the fight]. . . . Then he came to me as I was waiting. . . . Then he took his shield and his battleax and his armful of javelins. Now after I had let his weapons issue forth [without doing me any damage] . . . he charged me and I shot him, my arrow sticking in his neck. He cried out and fell on his nose. I [finished him off] with his own battleax and raised my cry of victory.[32]

Papyri and Libraries

Papyri, paper sheets or scrolls, were at least as abundant as ostraca as a writing medium in Egypt. This distinctive form of paper made from papyrus, a marsh plant native to Egypt, was widely exported to other Mediterranean lands throughout antiquity. The first-century-A.D. Roman scholar Pliny the Elder gave this description of how it was made:

Paper is manufactured from papyrus by splitting it [the plant's stem] with a needle into strips that are very thin but as long as possible. The quality of the papyrus is best at the center of the plant and decreases progressively toward the outsides. . . . All paper is "woven" on a board dampened with water from the Nile [to prevent the strips from drying out]; the muddy liquid acts as glue. First, an upright layer is smeared on the table—the whole length of the papyrus is used and both its ends are trimmed; then strips are laid across and complete a criss-cross pattern, which is then squeezed in presses. The sheets are dried in the sun and then joined together.[33]

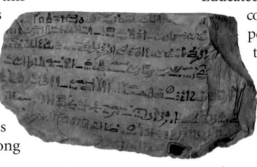

Dating from ca. 1250 B.C., this is one of the surviving ostraca bearing part of the famous Tale of Sinuhe.

This joining of the individual sheets was accomplished with glue. Then about twenty of the bound sheets were wound around a wooden dowel, making a roll usually twenty or thirty feet long. People wrote on the papyrus with a reed or bronze pen dipped in ink made from soot. Each roll, or "book," held roughly ten to twenty thousand words of text.

Papyri were the most versatile of the ancient writing mediums, and people used them to record all manner of literature, from letters and administrative lists to poetry and prose. Educated people and priests collected the scrolls like people collect books today, forming libraries of all sizes. Those private individuals who could afford to buy them stored them in jars in their homes, for example. The libraries in Egyptian temples were considerably larger. They were located in a section known as the House of Life, in which the copying of texts and the education of priests (and others) also took place. "The scribes of the House of Life were the 'servants' or 'followers' of Ra, the Sun god," Rosalie David points out. "Since this deity possessed the creative power to maintain life, it was appropriate that the scribes were believed to have the ability to express this creative power in their compositions."[34]

Occasionally in the ancient world, much larger numbers of scroll-books were collected in massive libraries maintained by the government. The biggest and most famous example was the renowned Great Library, erected in Alexandria, Egypt, by the first Greek pharaoh, Ptolemy I. He and the institution's first director, the Athenian scholar Demetrius Phalereus, sent agents to all parts of the known world to buy manuscripts, and the facility eventually boasted more than 700,000 papyrus scrolls. Scholars from far and wide utilized the Great Library, which also featured reading rooms and lecture halls. (Access to the books was restricted to these scholars and members of the government; public borrowing, the norm today, was not allowed and would have been pointless anyway, since so few ordinary people could read.)

Writing Systems

Whatever the medium used to convey written words, the Egyptians expressed those words in diverse ways, often depending on the age in which they were composed. The first of the several writing systems they developed—hieroglyphics (meaning "sacred signs")—appeared near the close of the Predynastic Period, perhaps about 3200 B.C. Hieroglyphics remained in use, alongside other writing systems, for more than three millennia. In pharaonic times, the system consisted of about a thousand picture signs. More were added later, especially in the Ptolemaic Pe-

A surviving New Kingdom book is written in hieroglyphics. Some of the picture-signs stood for objects, while others represented sounds.

These hieroglyphics were found in the tomb of the pharaoh Horemheb. The ovals in the center are cartouches containing the king's names.

riod, when there were nearly five thousand signs. The signs were normally read from right to left and top to bottom, and there was no punctuation or spaces between words. Combined with the large number of signs, this made hieroglyphics very difficult to read.

A number of hieroglyphic signs were diagrams (called logograms) that captured the main visual elements of the things being depicted. For instance, the sign for the sun was a circle with a dot in the middle, and the sign for a house was a rectangle representing a simple ground plan of a house. Other hieroglyphs called phonograms stood for spoken sounds. A squiggly horizontal line represented the sound of the letter *n*, and a snakelike symbol stood for the sound of *dj* or *z*.

Hieroglyphics were used to record many writing genres, but their main use was in funerary texts. Both literature and administrative records were more often recorded in the second oldest Egyptian writing system—hieratic. Developed in the Early Dynastic Period, hieratic was a script with some characters that were simplifications of common hieroglyphs. This script, which people read from right to left, remained in wide use until the Twenty-sixth Dynasty (664–525 B.C.).

A newer script that largely replaced hieratic at that time is known as demotic, the Greek word for it. The Egyptians called it *sekh shat*, meaning "writing for documents." And indeed at first, demotic, which originally developed from a dialect of spoken degree hieroglyphics and hieratic, continued to be used in the Ptolemaic Period. But not surprisingly, with a Greek dynasty then in power Greek became the main language of the royal court and official and legal documents. Most Egyptians still spoke the age-old native language, and the inability to speak, and especially to write, Greek proved a major barrier to many ordinary people who wanted to enter government service.

Finally, in late antiquity, when Christianity became widespread in Egypt, Coptic writing developed. The Coptic system, which used a script that combined some Greek letters and some demotic signs, was the main means by which the Egyptians read the Old and New Testaments.

Literary Genres: Funerary Texts and Hymns

It is not surprising that these Christian holy books became so important to the Egyptians following their conversion to Christianity. The Egyptians had always been extremely religiously devout. And religious texts, especially those dealing with death and the afterlife, had always constituted a major literary genre in the country.

The earliest surviving Egyptian funerary texts, today called the Pyramid Texts, were carved onto the interior walls of several pyramid tombs during the Old Kingdom. These writings convey much information about the proper ways for pharaohs and other royal persons to reach and prosper in the afterlife. One of these texts, "The Journey of the Deceased into

Egyptian common in the Nile Delta, was used mainly for commercial and administrative documents. Over time, however, it was also employed for literary, scientific, and religious texts.

Demotic was not the last Egyptian writing system that developed. It, and to a lesser the Sky," describes the resurrection of the pharaoh's soul from the tomb to meet and join with the sun god, Ra, in the sky:

> He flies away from you, you men. He is no longer in the Earth. He is in the sky. He rushes at the sky as a heron [large water bird]. He has kissed the sky as a hawk. . . . A ramp into the sky is built for him, that he may go up to the sky on it. . . . He flies as a bird, and he settles as a beetle on the empty seat on the [sky] ship of Ra. . . . He has gone up into the sky and has found Ra, who stands up when [the pharaoh] draws near. . . . He has taken his stand with Ra in the northern part of the sky.[35]

Another series of funerary texts, today referred to as the Coffin Texts, were written during the Middle Kingdom. Many of these writings were edited versions of the Pyramid Texts. The main difference was that the Coffin Texts recognized that all people, not just the pharaoh and nobles, could reach the afterlife and meet the gods. Some of the Coffin Texts include sayings intended to help a dead person navigate the uncertain paths in the afterlife.

Another important set of funerary texts, the Book of the Dead, appeared not long before the advent of the New Kingdom. Roughly half of the chants and spells in the volume came from the Pyramid and Coffin texts. Probably the best known section of the Book of the Dead is the one containing the so-called negative confession, which a deceased person supposedly recited to the god Osiris in hopes of being admitted into the Underworld. The negative confession read in part:

> I have not blasphemed [spoken against] a god. I have not robbed the poor. I have not done what the god abhors [hates]. . . . I have not caused tears. I have not killed. . . . I have not damaged the offerings in the temples. . . . I have not taken milk from the mouths of children.[36]

Hymns made up another crucial form of sacred literature. They were recited or sung during ceremonies conducted privately by priests in temples and by all worshippers in public religious festivals. Several examples have survived, the most famous of which is one composed by the pharaoh Akhenaten (reigned ca. 1352–1336 B.C.) to honor the god Aten, whom he envisioned as the blinding disk of the sun. "You appear beautifully on the horizon of heaven, you living Aten, the beginning of life!" the hymn begins.

> When you have risen on the eastern horizon, you fill every land with your beauty. You are gracious, great, glistening, and high over every land. . . . The world came into being by your hand. . . . One lives only through you.[37]

Other Important Literary Genres

Very few pharaohs actually composed verses as Akhenaten did. However, a large number of historical annals were written by scribes over the centuries in the names of various Egyptian kings, a great many of them commemorating and describing military campaigns. By accepted convention, they always claimed a victory, even when a battle ended in a defeat or draw. Often such annals were inscribed as running captions on relief sculptures on the walls of palaces. Among the more striking examples is one celebrating the victory of the great warrior-pharaoh Thutmose III (ca. 1479–1425 B.C.) over his enemies at Megiddo, in northern Palestine. "[The] command was given to the whole army," part of it reads,

> saying: "Equip yourselves! Prepare your weapons! for we shall advance to fight with that wretched foe in the morning!" . . . The watch[men] of the army went about, saying, "Steady of heart! Steady of heart! Watchful! Watchful! Watch for life at the tent of the king." . . . Early in the morning, behold, command was given to the entire army to move. His majesty went forth in a chariot of electrum, arrayed in his weapons of war, like [the god] Horus, the Smiter, lord of power.[38]

Not all Egyptian literature dealt with death, war, and conquest. There were also many love songs, most of which were written during the New Kingdom or later. In addition, large numbers of popular stories were composed, seemingly mainly to entertain people. Because most Egyptians could not read, it was common for a literate person to read a tale to a group; no doubt illiterate people then memorized stories and recited them to others, blending oral and written tradition.

In addition to the great Middle Kingdom story about the travels of Sinuhe, nu-

An illustration from the Book of the Dead depicts a person reciting the "negative confession" to Osiris, god of the Underworld.

A Surviving Treaty

Few examples of one important kind of official literature—the treaty—have survived from ancient Egypt. One notable exception is the treaty signed by the New Kingdom pharaoh Ramesses II and the king of the Hittites, ending a long period of warfare between the two peoples. The document (translated by A.H. Gardiner in an article for the Journal of Egyptian Archaeology*), reads in part:*

Behold, Hattusilis, the great chief of Hatti [land of the Hittites], has made himself in a treaty with [Ramesses], the great ruler of Egypt, beginning with this day, to cause to be made good peace and good brotherhood between us forever. . . . And the land of Egypt with the land of Hatti shall be at peace and in brotherhood . . . and hostilities shall not be made between them forever. And the great chief of Hatti shall not trespass into the land of Egypt; and the great ruler of Egypt shall not trespass into the land of Hatti. . . . And if another enemy come to the lands of the great ruler of Egypt, and he send to the great chief of Hatti saying, "Come with me as help against him," the great chief of Hatti shall come to him . . . [and help him] slay his enemy. . . . As for these words of the treaty . . . a thousand gods, male and female gods of those of the land of Hatti, together with [those] of Egypt—they are with me as witnesses hearing these words.

merous longer, more complex narratives appeared in the New Kingdom. Some had mythological themes and described the exploits of gods; others dealt with the adventures, troubles, and triumphs of ordinary humans. Some of the classic stories of the Late Period, written in demotic, including the *Tales of Setne* and *Cycle of Inaros*, may have been influenced by Greek epic poems like Homer's *Iliad* and *Odyssey*.

Finally, there were collections of philosophical sayings referred to as wisdom literature. One variety, called instruction, dealt mostly with proper and ethical behavior. An important example was the *Maxims of Ptahhotep*, supposedly composed by a Fifth Dynasty vizier of that name. Typical sayings from the work include "Do not be arrogant because of your knowledge, but confer with the ignorant man as with the learned," and "Do not inspire terror in men, for God also is repelled."[39] The other form of wisdom literature was discourse, which reflected on order and disorder in the world and how they might be reconciled. The existence and excellence of these philosophical literary forms shows that the Egyptians were occupied with much more than simple matters of subsistence, work, and funerary concerns. They were also concerned with right conduct, the nature of the world, and the place and fate of humankind in that world.

Chapter Seven

LEISURE GAMES AND SPORTS

The ancient Egyptians enjoyed a wide array of leisure activities and forms of entertainment, including both formal and informal sports and games. This is revealed by depictions in wall paintings and reliefs, papyri, and other descriptive sources, as well as by surviving examples of toys, game boards and pieces, and so forth.

All of this evidence, much of it discovered in the twentieth century, contradicts and corrects a belief held by many earlier modern scholars. As one of them put it, "The state of the common man [in Egypt] . . . must have been wretched in the extreme. . . . Wretched people, toiling people, do not play. . . . The Egyptians did not play."[40] This assessment was completely wrong. The Egyptians were far from an unhappy people, a fact attested to in one of the famous maxims attributed to the vizier Ptahhotep. "Be merry all your life," it begins. "Do no more than you are ordered to, nor shorten the time accorded to leisure. It is hateful to the spirit to be robbed of the time for merriment."[41] Following this

advice, members of both the upper and lower classes in Egypt played and pursued what leisure activities they could whenever possible.

The well-to-do, of course, did not have to work on a day-to-day basis, so they had more time available to amuse themselves. For this reason they staged, took part in, or watched most of the more organized and formal sporting contests. Among others, these included large-scale boat races (similar to those sponsored by modern yacht clubs) and ceremonial displays of target shooting. Even some of the pharaohs themselves engaged in both of these sports as well as others. This fact has come to light thanks to the survival of the so-called Archery Stela, set up by the pharaoh Amenhotep II in the fifteenth century B.C. It describes numerous sporting events staged by the nobles and is the single most important source of information about these activities.

Other ancient written sources, as well as various examples of archaeological evidence, show that the leisure activities pursued by members of the lower classes were usually less formal. Simple ball games and physical contests like tug-of-war were popular among farmers and laborers, for example. However, the well-to-do engaged in such activities, too. Many leisure pastimes were universal, regardless of one's level of wealth and social status.

Children's Toys and Games

This was especially true of children's toys and games. It appears that most Egyptians of all social classes played in largely the same ways when they were young. The main difference was that upper-class families could afford more and higher-quality toys, a fact of life in modern society as well.

Similarly, Egyptian children played with many of the same sorts of toys that modern children do, including dolls and puppets. Poorer families made dolls and puppets from simple, cheap materials such as clay or Nile silt, which might be left in the sun to dry or baked in an open fire or kiln. Members of the upper classes could afford well-crafted wooden versions, some with movable limbs. Whatever they were made of, the figurines represented ordinary people, dwarves, and a wide range of animals, including monkeys, donkeys, crocodiles, and hippopotamuses.

Other common children's toys included rattles, tops, and miniature weapons (swords, axes, bows and arrows, and chariots). And like children in all lands and times, Egyptian youngsters played with balls. In a surviving wall painting, two girls toss a small ball back and forth while their

These ancient Egyptian toys include a "paddle doll" with woolen hair (left) and a wooden cat.

friends clap their hands. This clapping seems to be an effort to maintain a rhythm. Other evidence indicates that it was common to combine ball playing and dance steps. Some Egyptian children (the actual percentage is unknown) learned to juggle several balls at once, as depicted in some tomb paintings. Another painted scene depicts some children interacting in pairs. One child in each pair carries the other in piggyback fashion while the ones on top throw a ball back and forth.

The latter game required strength and dexterity, and it and other acrobatic-style games were common in Egypt. That adults enjoyed watching children play them is revealed by a series of carved reliefs in the tombs of some Old Kingdom viziers. One child is shown riding piggyback on another, scholar Vera Olivova writes, while

> a boy is balancing on the shoulders of four others, and another is leaping high in the air, a feat still popular with Egyptian children today. . . . Scenes of this kind are accompanied by inscriptions like "Hold tight!" and "Look out, I'm coming!" A common game was for a file [line] of boys to pass the stiff body of one of their number back over their heads, and another, for several children holding hands to spin around in a circle. There are also illustrations of a tug-of-war between two teams of three children, of a game with one child in the middle of a ring trying to catch one of the others by the feet, and of boys . . . sitting back-to-back with arms linked, trying to pull each other over.[42]

Board Games

Not all Egyptian games involved physical exertion. Like the ancient Greeks and Romans, as well as millions of people today, both children and adults in Egypt enjoyed playing parlor games, specifically board games. Perhaps the most popular Egyptian board game was *senet*, roughly translated as "passing." The game required a grid of squares and several small game pieces that were at least superficially similar to those used in modern checkers and chess. People of poor or moderate means scratched or painted a grid on the surface of a flat stone or piece of wood and used small rocks or bones for game pieces. The wealthy had elaborate, finely crafted wooden boards, often inlaid with ivory, and carved wooden game pieces.

The evidence for the game is fairly extensive. Four intact *senet* boards, each with game pieces, were found in King Tut's tomb, and other wealthy tombs have yielded several more. The game is also frequently depicted in paintings on walls and papyrus scrolls. One papyrus scene, dating from circa 1150 B.C. and obviously meant to be humorous, shows a lion and antelope playing *senet*. Unfortunately, even though these boards, game pieces, and painted depictions have survived, the exact rules and strategies of the game have not. However, modern scholars have pieced together what appear to have been the basics of the game. "The two players each had an equal number of pieces," Ian Shaw suggests,

> usually seven, distinguished by shape or color, and they played on a grid of thirty

squares known as *perw* ("houses") and arranged in three rows of ten. Moves were determined by "throw-sticks" or knucklebones [dicelike pieces of wood or bone]. The object was to convey the pieces around a snaking [winding] track to the finish, via a number of specially marked squares representing good or bad fortune.[43]

A number of other board games were popular in Egypt as well, several of which involved two people who faced each other across a playing board. One of these games, *taw*, introduced by foreign invaders in the late Middle Kingdom, used a board with twenty squares, arranged in three rows (of four, twelve, and four squares). In contrast, up to six people could play *mehen*, the "snake" or "serpent" game. *Mehen* used game pieces in the shape of lions, dogs, and balls. Still another popular parlor game had pieces shaped like the heads of jackals, dogs, and other animals. Even less is known about the rules for these games than is known about those for *senet*.

Kingly Games

Like other Egyptians, the pharaohs enjoyed playing *senet* and other parlor games. But these monarchs were equally, if not more, fond of exerting themselves in physical displays that modern heads of state would not dare to attempt. Some shot their bows at targets while charging forward on moving chariots. The inscription on a carved relief showing Amenhotep II doing this reads:

Entering his northern garden, he saw that four targets of Asian copper had been set up for him, as thick as a man's palm, and the distance between one target-post and the next was twenty ells [about thirty-three feet]. Then his majesty appeared on his war chariot like Montu [a war god] in all his might. He bent his bows and seized the arrows at once. Then he started up his chariot and shot at all four targets, like Montu in all his glory. His arrow sped through one target and hit the next post. He let fly his arrow at the copper target so that it came out of it again and fell to the ground—a deed no one else had performed and of which no one had ever heard. . . . His Majesty performed these feats before the eyes of the whole land.[44]

The last claim—about performing before the "whole land"—is a bit deceiving because the pharaoh did not put on exhibitions for the laborers and other peasants. Only courtiers, wealthy aristocrats, and higher-ranking soldiers had the privilege of watching the king perform this way.

Another sport that Amenhotep II pursued was extremely popular among the Egyptian nobles—rowing. One inscription claims:

His arms were so strong, that he was never faint when he grasped the oar and rowed his arrow-swift ship, the best of the crew of two-hundred. Many were faint after a course of half a mile, exhausted and weary of limb and out of shape; but His Majesty still rowed powerfully with his [oar], laying his oar aside and bringing his ship to shore only after all had seen what he had done.[45]

Such depictions of pharaohs greatly outperforming even the strongest of their subjects were partly intended as propaganda. There is no reason to believe that any of the Egyptian kings were physical supermen. Rather, it was customary in Egyptian

A carved relief shows men enjoying water jousting. Other water sports were popular in ancient Egypt, including swimming and shooting the rapids.

art to bolster rulers' images by making them look physically (as well as mentally) superior to other people.

Water Sports

Amenhotep's rowing exhibitions constitute only one of many examples of water sports in ancient Egypt. Maybe because of the ready availability of the Nile River, Red Sea, Mediterranean Sea, and the country's many irrigation canals, people of all walks of life enjoyed sports and games that involved water. It appears that most Egyptians could swim, and scribes developed a special hieroglyph that stood for swimming. There was even a goddess of swimming named Wadjet. In addition, from the New Kingdom on, craftsmen commonly depicted people swimming in the artifacts they produced; some spoons from that era, for example, have swimming girls carved onto the handles.

Water sports involving boats were equally popular. The rich staged boat races. And common people enjoyed "water jousting," which usually utilized small riverboats made from bundled plant stems. Each of the opposing boats (of which there might be two or more) had a crew that included one or more oarsmen and one "fighter," who stood upright and wielded a long stick. While the oarsmen moved the vessels to and fro, attempting to gain whatever advantage they could, the fighters swung their sticks at one another. When a fighter was knocked into the water, his boat was eliminated, and the last boat left with a standing fighter was the winner.

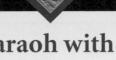

A Pharaoh with No Equal?

It was customary in the New Kingdom to issue official propaganda that made the pharaohs appear to be superior physical specimens who excelled at sports and war. Typical is this passage from a stele erected by Amenhotep II (translated in Vera Olivova's book about ancient sports), which touts that pharaoh's physical achievements.

His Majesty ascended the throne as a young man in full command of his body. At eighteen he was peerless in courage and knew all the ways of Montu [a war god], so that he had no equal in war, and he understood horses, so that he had no equal among many soldiers. Nor was there anyone who could bend a bow like him, and no one excelled him in running against others. His arms were so strong, that he was never faint when he grasped the oar and rowed his arrow-swift ship, the best of the crew of two-hundred. Many were faint after a course of half a mile, exhausted and weary of limb and out of shape; but His Majesty still rowed powerfully with his [oar], laying his oar aside and bringing his ship to shore only after all had seen what he had done. He also bent three hundred strong bows and compared the work of the bow makers, telling the good craftsmen from the bad.

The first-century-A.D. Roman playwright Seneca the Younger, who owned land in Egypt in the Roman Period, described a considerably more dangerous water sport: shooting the Nile's rapids. These rapids occur only at the river's cataracts. Cataracts are places where the ground level abruptly changes, forming areas of unusually turbulent currents and waves. In Seneca's words, a cataract was

> a remarkable spectacle [where the water] surges through rocks which are steep and jagged in many places, and unleashes its forces . . . in a violent torrent [that] leaps forward through narrow passages. . . . Finally, it struggles

through the obstructions in its way, and then, suddenly losing its support, falls down an enormous depth with a tremendous crash that echoes through the surrounding regions.[46]

Fascinated and delighted, Seneca spent many hours sitting and watching native Egyptians challenge the rapids, and fortunately he recorded what he saw for posterity. They "embark on small boats, two to a boat, and one rows while the other bails out water," he wrote.

> Then they are violently tossed about in the raging rapids. . . . At length they reach the narrowest channels . . . and,

One of the paintings from Beni Hasan shows wrestlers grappling. All of the moves portrayed are employed by modern wrestlers.

swept along by the whole force of the river, they control the rushing boat by hand and plunge head downward to the great terror of the onlookers. You would believe sorrowfully that by now they were drowned and overwhelmed by such a mass of water, when far from the place where they fell, they shoot out as from a catapult, still sailing, and the subsiding wave does not submerge them, but carries them on to smooth waters.[47]

The Oldest Sport: Wrestling

There is little doubt that swimming, boating, and some other water sports were among the oldest in Egypt, as well as in most other ancient lands. But as near as modern scholars can reckon, the oldest sport of all was wrestling. It was certainly the most popular and widely played of all ancient Egyptian sporting events.

Wrestling is also one of the most unchanging sports in the historical annals. If a skilled Egyptian (or Greek or Roman) wrestler could somehow transport himself to the modern world, he would have no trouble at all adapting to today's wrestling styles. The evidence for this is overwhelming. At Beni Hasan, for example, archaeologists found a series of more than four hundred Middle Kingdom paintings depicting men wrestling. These athletes employed many of the same moves and holds used by modern wrestlers, both amateur and professional. The figures in the paintings apply classic headlocks, armlocks, and bodylocks; trips; shoulder throws; flying mares; and many other common wrestling moves.

The "dirty fighting" rampant in modern professional wrestling is also evident in ancient Egyptian depictions of the sport. The Beni Hasan renderings show wrestlers choking each other, for instance. It is unclear whether choking was legal or illegal in Egyptian wrestling, but it seems to have been frowned on at the least. A later Egyptian sculpture of a wrestling exhibition at the royal court shows a fighter applying a choke hold; an accompanying inscription reads, "Take care! You are in the presence of the Pharaoh!"[48]

The paintings at Beni Hasan and others like them reveal that Egyptian wrestling had other features similar to those of modern versions of the game. Egyptian matches were overseen by referees, for example. Also, at least some Egyptian grapplers employed psychological tactics designed to make their opponents nervous and fearful. A wrestler in one painting taunts another with phrases such as "I'm going to pin you! I'll make you weep in your heart and cringe with fear. Look, I'm going to make you fall and faint away right in front of the Pharaoh!"[49]

Wrestling and other combat sports became especially popular in the New Kingdom because this was the era when Egypt embarked on large-scale conquests in Palestine, Syria, and elsewhere. The army became more organized and professional. And combat sports became part of the soldiers' official training regimen. These activities then spilled over into nonmilitary life as the soldiers and their friends and offspring participated in combat sports in friendly competitions. In addition to wrestling, boxing, and stick fighting (with

Dinner Parties

One leisure pastime that seems to have been mainly the province of the well-to-do in ancient Egypt was giving and attending parties. Brooklyn Museum scholar James F. Romano discusses this in his book describing daily life in Egypt.

Among the aristocracy, formal banquets provided an opportunity for feasting, drink, music, and conversation. Scantily clad maidens offered guests carefully prepared [food] and drinks and poured water over their hands [to clean them] when necessary. For the occasion, the hosts brought out their most impressive tableware, including finely crafted stone and faience drinking goblets and highly polished metal vessels. Occasionally the celebrants overindulged. Two New Kingdom wall paintings show unfortunate party guests no longer able to hold down their food.

A wall painting found in a tomb shows guests enjoying themselves at a banquet.

the sticks substituting for the swords and clubs used in real combat) were popular.

In examining the evidence for these ancient activities, one cannot help but be struck by the similarities to modern ones. Boxing, wrestling, swimming, rowing, and playing board games and ball games are still among the most popular leisure activities. This shows that, despite a number of pronounced differences between the cultures of ancient Egypt and the modern world, at least in their methods of play people have changed very little in the course of thousands of years.

Chapter Eight

HUNTING AND FISHING

Among the most widespread of the leisure activities the ancient Egyptians engaged in were hunting and fishing. Because both were also at times practical ways to procure food, they deserve to be considered separately from those leisure pastimes intended mainly for relaxation and amusement. In fact, both hunting and fishing originated as food-gathering activities far back in the Stone Age, when they were the only means of getting meat. In late Neolithic times and on into the Predynastic Period, however, the people of the Nile Valley adopted agriculture and the raising of livestock. And domestic breeding of animals steadily replaced hunting as a means of acquiring meat. This was particularly true for members of the upper classes, for whom hunting and fishing increasingly became traditional leisure rituals and pursuits. The same can be said for many Egyptians of average means. However, for poor people fish remained an important source of protein,

as well as a leisure activity, until the end of antiquity and well beyond.

Although all ancient societies engaged in hunting and fishing mostly for these same reasons, in Egypt these activities were colored to some degree by a rather unique view of animals. From the country's earliest days, the people lived in close proximity to animals, keeping them not only in pens and cages but often in their homes. "They live with their animals," Herodotus wrote after his extended visit to Egypt, "unlike [people in] the rest of the world, who live apart from them."[50] Not surprisingly, this proximity sometimes led human caretakers to bond with their animals. "Those who kept animals knew them well," Eugen Strouhal points out, including

their mating habits, their diet and growth, their ailments, and all their characteristics. They took pleasure in breeding them successfully, but did not see them merely as utilities. We know

This nineteenth-century woodcut illustrates the close interaction and spiritual connection between humans and animals in ancient Egypt.

from many illustrations what [good] care they took of them. When a flock had to ford a canal or creek, the shepherds would pick up the little ones gently in their arms and carry them across. We can see them stroking an animal's muzzle when feeding it. . . . We can even see a farmer feeding a piglet from his own mouth.[51]

In fact, though they remained meat eaters, the Egyptians developed a sort of unwritten moral code about the humane and ethical treatment of animals. This consideration remained largely unknown in most parts of the world until the appearance of organizations like the SPCA (Society for the Prevention of Cruelty to Animals) in modern times.

Philosophically, the Egyptians did not separate themselves from animals and the rest of nature to the degree that other ancient peoples did (including the Greeks and Romans). To the Egyptians, humans, animals, and plants were, both spiritually and practically speaking, all part of a greater natural whole. Therefore, the Egyptians approached hunting and fishing, even for sport, with feelings of thankfulness, reverence, and respect for their prey that most modern hunters would not understand or appreciate.

Early Game and Hunting Methods

What the early Egyptian hunters themselves may not have appreciated fully was how fortunate they were in the abundance of game available to them. In Neolithic times and throughout much of the Predynastic Period, human settlements were fewer and more widely separated. Also, the climate was somewhat wetter and a great deal of thick marshland, even some stretches of jungle, existed along the Nile and some of its tributaries. These moist woodlands were populated with large numbers of game, including some that could be termed big game. Giraffes and elephants still roamed, as did rhinoceroses and wild boar. Crocodiles and hippopotamuses teemed in the waterways. And the narrow but fertile grasslands bordering the river supported considerable populations of lions, leopards, hyenas, ostriches, gazelles, antelope, and multitudes of bird species.

The hunters stalked these creatures in a variety of ways. Bows and arrows were common for attacking from a distance, as was a rock attached to the end of a rope and thrown (similar to the South American bolas). Spears, swords, knives, and clubs could be used for closer work, and slings were employed to bring down birds. Sometimes dogs or human runners drove antelope or other less dangerous beasts into fenced enclosures, after which some of the captured animals were killed and eaten while others were kept on farms or in homes.

This hunters' paradise eroded rather rapidly in late Predynastic times and during the Old Kingdom. First, much of North Africa was in the final stages of a drying trend, and Egypt in general became more arid. Second, and no less eventful, human settlements and their cultivated farmlands expanded, driving many of the larger animal species out. Some remained in low-lying swamps and in the marshy reaches of the Nile Delta. But others disappeared altogether.

A painting from the tomb of a New Kingdom scribe and priest named Nakht shows him and members of his family hunting in the marshes.

Royal Hunting Expeditions

By the time the pharaohs began launching hunting expeditions in the Old Kingdom, therefore, the numbers of species and individual animals available had significantly declined. The problem became even more pronounced by the advent of the New Kingdom when such royal hunts became very large-scale and extravagant. As a result, it became common practice for the king's game wardens to stock a large enclosed area with beasts and allow him and his noble guests to roam the area at will. By the New Kingdom, elephants and most lions, as well as several other big game species, had to be imported from foreign lands to stock the royal hunting preserves.

Several visual and written accounts of these royal hunts have survived. Some conducted by Amenhotep III (reigned 1390–1352 B.C.) were captured in carvings on scarab jewelry. They show detailed scenes of the pharaoh chasing wild bulls and lions. A caption in another hunting scene depicting the same ruler boasts that "the total number of lions killed by His Majesty with his own arrows, from the first to the tenth year [of his reign], was 102 wild lions." A longer inscription reads:

His Majesty mounted a chariot drawn by a team of horses and the whole army went with him. Both the commander and the rank and file, as well as the people of the region, had been told to keep watch on the herd of wild cattle. His Majesty then ordered that the herd should be enclosed inside a fence with only one free way out. His Majesty then ordered them to count the herd. Their number was one hundred and seventy head of cattle. And on that day His

A painting on the lid of a chest from the tomb of King Tut shows the young pharaoh hunting desert animals from his chariot.

Majesty's bag [number of creatures captured] was fifty-six head.[52]

Another royal hunter, Thutmose III, bragged that he killed 120 elephants. An inscription accompanying a relief depicting the hunt reads, "No king has ever done such a thing since the world began!"[53] During this expedition, Thutmose nearly lost his life. According to the official account, after he hit one elephant with an arrow the elephant became enraged and charged at him. At the last second, one of the king's soldiers dashed forward and sheared off the beast's trunk, saving the pharaoh from certain death. Thus, even when they were corralled and to some degree controlled, some hunted animals remained quite dangerous.

Hunting from Chariots

It also became customary in the New Kingdom for pharaohs and other high-placed persons to hunt from moving chariots. A famous royal hunting scene of the era, carved outside the great temple at Medinet Habu (near Thebes), shows Ramesses III standing on his chariot and thrusting a spear at a wild bull. (In a lower register, several of his troops fire arrows at birds.) Still another chariot hunter, Userhet, a leading scribe under Amenhotep II, can be seen pursuing gazelles in a well-preserved painting in Userhet's tomb (in western Thebes). In a similar vein, a royal doctor, Nebamun, hunts hyenas in a scene painted on a wall in his own tomb.

When such a nobleman hunted by chariot, an expert driver operated the vehicle, which allowed the hunter to wield his weapons with both hands. This was especially important in the case of the bow and arrow, which simply cannot be operated with just one hand. An exciting scene in the 1954 film *The Egyptian* shows the future pharaoh Horemheb firing an arrow from a moving chariot and successfully dispatching a lion while someone else drives the chariot.

The popularity of hunting from chariots among New Kingdom royals is well illustrated by the discovery of six full-sized chariots in King Tut's tomb. Other hunting items found in the tomb include 46 bows, 427 arrows, 2 bronze swords, 2 gold daggers, 8 shields, and 2 slings. These artifacts leave no doubt that the boy king was an avid hunter. (Interestingly, Tut may have died after falling from his chariot during a hunt. Studies of his remains indicate an injury to the back of his head and a possible crushed breastbone, both consistent with such a fall.)

Common Fishing Methods

Noblemen, as well as ordinary Egyptians, also eagerly pursued fishing as a sport, especially in the Old and Middle kingdoms. During and after these eras, those who caught fish for the fun of it were distinct from the professional fishermen who caught fish for a living. Whether they did so for fun or economic necessity, the fishermen used a small number of tried-and-true methods. One early technique was to stand up in a boat and jab a harpoonlike spear at the fish as they swam by. The age-old rod and line were also commonly employed. The hooks at the ends of such a line were at first made of bone, which a fisherman carved to the desired sharpness. Later, metal hooks (mostly of copper or bronze) became common. (Reels and other modern-style casting equipment were unknown.)

The more elaborate means of catching fish in ancient Egypt included traps and dragnets. The traps were most often made from interwoven reed stems and resembled baskets. Just as modern fishermen do, an Egyptian angler lowered his trap on a rope to the bottom of the waterway in which he was fishing and marked the spot with a buoy (made of a lightweight wood that floated). A relief in the tomb of one nobleman shows fishermen using such a trap. "Pull hard on the oars so that we can get on top of them [the fish]!" one man says. After raising their trap, a colleague exclaims, "Full to the brim! This time we've done it!"[54]

Also as remains true today, dragnets brought in the biggest catches of fish. Strouhal describes the ancient technique, which some Egyptian fishermen still employ:

Clay, stone, or metal weights were fastened along one edge so that the net moved over the river bottom while the other side was kept at surface level with wooden floats. Reliefs show such a net being hauled along by anything from three to six men in two boats alongside one another, with another two [men] rowing for all they are worth.[55]

Egyptian Hippos

Among the large animals hunted in ancient Egypt was the hippopotamus, the Egyptian version of which the Greek historian Herodotus described in his Histories, *composed after he visited the country in the fifth century* B.C.

The hippopotamus ... has four legs, cloven hoofs like an ox, a snub nose, a horse's mane and tail, conspicuous tusks, a voice like a horse's neigh, and is about the size of a very large ox. Its hide is so thick and tough that when dried it can be made into spear-shafts.

A faience figurine from the late New Kingdom depicts a common target of hunters—the hippopotamus.

These wooden models found in a Middle Kingdom tomb show fishermen casting nets. Even the stone net weights are clearly depicted.

Fishing Dangers and Taboos

These fishing methods and scenes seem fairly familiar today. But there were other aspects of fishing in ancient Egypt that might seem somewhat strange to most modern anglers. First, by the advent of the New Kingdom it was not unusual for well-to-do people to create small artificial fish ponds on their property. A person might sit in a comfortable chair for hours beside such a pond, hoping for a bite. This was a far cry from the true sport that required a fisherman to brave the elements in the sea, a river, a lake, or a large canal.

Sometimes those who did fish in the traditional manner faced real dangers in these waterways, including a catfish armed with a poisonous spine in its top fin. This fish was so lethal that even crocodiles kept their distance from it. Speaking of crocodiles, these ferocious beasts constantly lurked in most of Egypt's waterways, waiting for unwary animals and humans to stray close enough to make a convenient meal. A piece of wisdom literature from the Middle Kingdom describes a fisherman who falls prey to the dreaded reptile:

And now I will tell you about the fisherman who . . . [plies his trade on] a river infested with crocodiles. When the time comes to count up [the fish caught that day], he wrings his hands, without even thinking, "There might

Of Ponds and Fish Eggs

During his visit to Egypt, Herodotus observed numerous locals at work in a wide variety of professions. Among these were fishermen. The Greek historian noted that they often fished in small ponds and marshes that filled up during the season when the Nile flooded, and in his Histories *he offered the following explanation for how fish got into these waterways.*

No sooner are these low-lying bits of ground formed into lakes than they are found to contain a multitude of fish. I think I understand the probable reason for this. . . . When the river is falling the previous year, [the fish] lay their eggs in the mud just before they get away with the last of the water, so that when the flood comes round again in due course, the eggs at once hatch and produce the fish.

This nineteenth-century woodcut depicts Egyptian fishermen and their families interacting on the riverbank.

be a crocodile around!" Too late he is gripped with fear. . . . As soon as he reaches the water he falls [to the crocodile's attack] as if struck by the hand of god.[56]

There were also some odd religious taboos regarding fish in Egypt. Some fish were viewed as sacred in particular regions of the land, yet the same fish were taboo in other regions. Part of this stemmed from the famous myth of Osiris, in which the evil god Seth cut up the body of the good god Osiris and some of these parts were eaten by various fish. One of these fish was the oxyrhynchus, a common Nile species. In the town and region of Oxyrhynchus (in central Egypt), this fish was held sacred because it was thought to carry some of Osiris's own flesh. At the same time, however, many Egyptians saw such fish as unclean because they had helped the evil Seth dispose of poor Osiris. The result of this belief was that pharaohs and priests were not allowed to eat any kind of fish, although they could still catch them.

The taboos regarding the eating of fish by certain people were not the only extreme rules relating to animals in Egypt. Hunting and killing certain animals was also taboo. Killing a household cat was seen as a serious crime, for instance. And Herodotus wrote: "For killing an ibis or a hawk, whether deliberately or not, the penalty is inevitably death."[57] The reasons for the extreme nature of such punishments and the deeply held feelings that fueled their creation are not entirely clear. But for comparison one can imagine how the average modern American or European would react to someone hunting down and eating someone's pet dog. In this and other ways, therefore, for the Egyptians hunting and fishing were not only means of sustenance and leisure but could be ethical and highly emotional issues as well.

Chapter Nine

MUSIC, SINGING, AND DANCING

A large number of surviving ancient Egyptian paintings and reliefs show people playing instruments, singing, and dancing. Some of these are visually stunning and stylistically unusual. One early New Kingdom painting, for example, includes two musicians whose faces are shown from the front in a realistic pose that breaks the Egyptian artistic rule of showing people's heads in profile. Along with the numerous musical instruments archaeologists have recovered (mostly from tombs), these visual images indicate that music was integral to Egyptian life, in both formal, serious settings and informal leisure activities.

Indeed, music and dancing were a basic part of a wide range of activities, including religious festivals, funerals, royal coronations, dinner parties, weddings, courting rituals, and victory celebrations. In addition, it was common for laborers to sing while they worked (especially when they worked in gangs) and for people to sing or play music to cheer up sick relatives and friends. The universality and widespread love of music in ancient Egypt, as well as the Egyptians' wry sense of humor, is well illustrated by a painting found on a papyrus (now on display in the Egyptian Museum in Turin, Italy). It shows a small musical band in which the instruments are played by a donkey, a lion, a crocodile, and a monkey.

Wind Instruments

As this humorous painting and other ancient images indicate, the basis of music (and indirectly of singing and dancing) in Egypt was the playing of musical instruments. Artistic renderings of people playing rudimentary instruments date back to Neolithic times, and a wide range of sophisticated musical instruments were depicted in the art of pharaonic times. Probably many ancient Egyptians could play one instrument or another well enough to plunk out a tune. But as has been the case in every society, only a few had the natural gift and the time necessary to become truly proficient. Therefore, a small class of professional musicians, whose social status was comparable to craftsmen, developed.

The instruments these musicians played can be conveniently grouped into three general categories. One consisted of wind in-struments, or instruments that people played by blowing into them. Of these, the oldest seems to have been the flute. The earliest versions were fashioned from reeds or pieces of wood hollowed out, but eventually metal flutes became common, too. They came in many different sizes, and it is probable that the longer ones could produce deeper, mellower tones than the shorter ones. An Old Kingdom relief shows a person playing a

A nineteenth-century English painting depicts musicians and a dancer entertaining Egyptian royalty.

This early New Kingdom painting of Egyptian musicians playing at a banquet is unusual because the faces of two of them are shown frontally.

flute roughly three feet long and blowing into it through one end. In the New Kingdom it became customary to close off the end and to blow into an opening in the side of the instrument, as is the case with modern flutes. Modern Egyptians still play a flute called the *uffafa*, which is very similar to the ones depicted in ancient art.

Modern Egyptians also play a clarinet-like reed instrument called a *zummara* that looks almost identical to clarinets used in Egypt from the early Old Kingdom on. (Reed instruments are those that utilize a thin piece of wood or plant fiber, which vi-brates when the player blows on it.) The double flute, or *aulos* (its Greek name), was introduced by the Greeks in the Late Period or Ptolemaic Period. There was also a double-reed instrument similar to a modern oboe, which the Egyptians borrowed from Asia Minor sometime during the New Kingdom. Still another wind instrument (today part of the brass family) was the trumpet, which may have originated as a signaling device in battle. Two exquisite gold and silver trumpets were found in King Tut's tomb. Some Egyptian musicians also blew through animal horns of various sizes; these were undoubtedly similar to the shofar, an ancient Hebrew instrument made from a ram's horn and still played today in some Jewish rituals.

Other Common Instruments

A second general family of instruments prevalent in ancient Egypt were string instruments that one plucked with the fingers. Because these were capable of playing chords (groups of three or more notes that sound at the same time), they are sometimes called cordophones. Probably the earliest string instrument in Egypt was the harp, which appeared in the Old Kingdom and may have been borrowed from Mesopotamia. It had from eleven to thirteen strings. And the player either knelt or stood to play it, depending on its height.

In the New Kingdom, several other string instruments came into use. One was a small, curved harp, a well-preserved example of which can be seen today in the Louvre Museum in Paris. Another was a lute, an early version of the guitar, which had a long neck and an oval body made of wood and covered by leather. (The sounds made by plucking the strings resonated inside the hollow wooden body.) There was also a small hand-held harp—the lyre—the Egyptian version of which had seven strings.

The third general category of musical instruments in Egypt was the percussion group. Percussion instruments are generally those that are hit, tapped, or shaken, often to keep the beat. One of the earliest of these was a set of ivory clappers that the player either smacked together or rapped against his or her body. Another percussion instrument, the *sistrum*, appears to have originated in Egypt. Eugen Strouhal describes it as "a hand-rattle with free-moving metal strips strung on a series of horizontal wires."[58] The metal strips clashed

A modern drawing based on ancient paintings shows women holding typical ancient Egyptian instruments, including an aulos *and a harp.*

and vibrated like miniature cymbals. Larger cymbals, about five to seven inches in diameter and attached to a player's hand, were introduced into Egypt during the Late Period. Drums, played by striking them with the hand instead of a stick or mallet, were also common.

One instrument that did not fit into these general categories but became widely popular in Egypt in late antiquity was invented by an Alexandrian Greek, Ctesibius, in the third century B.C. Called the *hydraulos*, it was essentially a large organ that made sounds when someone pumped air into it using a bellows. The instrument had a rudimentary keyboard and a loud, arresting sound that made it popular in large-scale public venues such as at festivals, coronations, and athletic games. (The Romans used a version of it to provide background music for gladiatorial bouts.)

Songs of Reverence

In Egypt, and elsewhere in the ancient world, musicians invariably accompanied singers. In fact, people sang at nearly every conceivable public occasion, as well as at private gatherings and while they worked. Some modern scholars have attempted to reconstruct what these songs sounded like, but the Egyptians had no musical notation (written notes to guide the musicians and singers), so there is no sure way to know what kinds of scales, melodies, and harmonies were employed. It appears that a pentatonic scale (one having five tones, or notes) was in use before and during the Old Kingdom and that a heptatonic scale (with seven tones) came into use later. Either scale can produce a wide range of musical styles (as different from one another as a classical harpsichord sonata is from a heavy metal rock song). And discerning which style was prevalent in ancient Egypt is difficult, if not impossible.

What *has* survived and tells modern observers a great deal about the intent and spirit of Egyptian music are the lyrics, or words, to many songs. Because the Egyptians were so devoutly religious (as Herodotus remarked, "religious to excess, beyond any other nation in the world"[59]), many of their songs were connected to worship.

"My Girl"

This is the seventh of the Songs of the City of Memphis, *a collection of surviving New Kingdom love songs (quoted in W.K. Simpson's* Literature of Ancient Egypt*). It is about a young man who thinks he does not see enough of his girlfriend and would be willing to endure her anger if that was the only way to spend time with her.*

Back at the farmstead of my girl[friend], the doorway in the center of the house, her door [could be] left ajar [so that I could get into her room], [but] her door bolt [is] sprung [broken]. My girl is furious! If I were made the doorkeeper, I could make her mad at me. Then at least I'd hear her voice when she's angry, and I'd play the child afraid of her.

For example, out of a sense of awe, reverence, and thankfulness they sang to one of their most important deities, Ra, the chief sun god. Every morning a group of women at the royal court (and likely many private groups and individuals as well) sang the "Morning Hymn to the Sun," which went in part:

> Awake in peace, you Cleansed One, in peace! . . . You sleep in the bark [boat] of the evening, you awake in the bark of the morning, for you are he that soars above the [other] gods. There is no other god that soars over you![60]

Similarly, priests chanted various religious songs when going about their sacred duties in temples. And crowds of worshippers chanted as they marched in (or watched) religious processions in which priests carried images of the gods from one temple to another.

For the Egyptians, the Nile's life-giving qualities made that river a quasi-religious entity. And shortly before the advent of the New Kingdom a religious festival that celebrated the river's yearly inundation (gentle flood that irrigated crops) featured the "Hymn to the Nile." "Praise to you, O Nile," it began,

> that issues forth from the earth and comes to nourish the dwellers in Egypt . . . that waters the meadows that Ra has created to nourish all cattle, that gives drink to the desert places that are far from water. . . . Controller of the corn-god that makes every workshop

> [flourish] . . . lord of fish that makes the water fowl go upstream . . . that makes barley and creates wheat . . . bringer of nourishment, plenteous of sustenance, creating all things good.[61]

Songs Honoring the Pharaoh

While some songs were clearly religious in nature, others were more secular. Of the latter, many had political motivations and overtones. Just as modern American bands and singers greet the U.S. president with "Hail to the Chief" or "America the Beautiful," ancient Egyptians broke into song to celebrate public appearances of the pharaohs. The following song was composed in honor of the arrival of a pharaoh at a town near the capital of Memphis:

> How great is the Lord for his city!
>
>> He is [allied with, or one and the same with] Ra and other rulers of men are insignificant.
>
> How great is the Lord for his city!
> Yes, he is a dam which holds back the river against its floodwaters.
>
> How great is the Lord for his city!
> Yes, he is a cool place that lets every man sleep till daybreak. . . .
>
> How great is the Lord for his city!
>
>> Yes, he is a mountain that wards off the storm at the time of tempest.[62]

Another kind of political song honoring the king was the hymn of victory, sung

A nineteenth-century woodcut captures the festive atmosphere created by musicians and dancers for one of the pharaohs.

in lavish ceremonies following military campaigns. This example dates to the mid–New Kingdom and honored the pharaoh Eptahmern (reigned ca. 1213–1203 B.C.) after his defeat of the Libyans:

> Great joy has come to Egypt. . . . How amiable is he, the victorious ruler! How magnified is the king among the gods! How fortunate is he, the commanding lord! . . . One comes and goes with singing, and there is no lamentation of mourning people. . . . The [enemy] kings are overthrown. . . . Not one [of them] holds up his head. . . . Kheta [land of the Hittites] is pacified . . . Israel is desolated. Syria is made a widow for Egypt.[63]

Love Songs

On a personal level, the Egyptians produced numerous love songs, a large number of which have survived. Most of these were written during the New Kingdom or later, and the majority were likely accompanied by a solo instrument (although some may have had the benefit of larger ensembles of musicians). Some of these songs are quite passionate—in fact, no less so than many modern ones—and show that romantic love was not uncommon among Egyptian men and women. The following example, from a group of songs sometimes called *Songs of the City of Memphis*, is a case in point:

> My love for you is mixed throughout my body like [salt] dipped in water . . .

like milk shot through [water]. . . . So hurry to see your lady, like a stallion on the track, or like a falcon [swooping down] to its papyrus marsh. Heaven sends down the love of her as a flame falls in the hay.[64]

Even more passionate, as well as rather modern sounding, is this verse of another love song: "I turn around toward love of you when I am by myself again. My heart is balanced with your heart. I cannot [bear to] be far from all this beauty."[65] One can only imagine how moving these words must have sounded when accompanied by melodic music.

Dancers and Dancing

Where there was music and singing in ancient Egypt, there was almost always dancing, too. As ancient paintings and figurines show, some form of dancing accompanied religious worship, feasts and parties, funeral rites, military exercises and celebrations, and many other occasions. Both men and women danced, but never together, as is widely common today. Also, most major group dancing in public displays seems to have been done by women.

The Egyptians did not draw a clear line between the disciplines of dancing and acrobatics (or gymnastics). And it was not unusual to see dancers performing handstands, spins, and cartwheels, somewhat similar to modern break-dancers. According to Strouhal:

Scenes that have survived show, for example, groups of girls spinning round,

Love in the Garden

This unusual Egyptian love song (quoted in Mayer and Prideaux's Never to Die*) is sung from the point of view of a tree in the garden of a beautiful maiden. The tree's love for the maiden, who planted it, symbolizes the deep, faithful, long-lasting kind of love that has been the romantic ideal in every age.*

The fig tree utters its voice, [and] its foliage comes, saying: "I will be a servant to the mistress. Is there any so noble as I? Yet if you have no slave I am the servant brought from Syria as booty for the beloved. She caused me to be set in her orchard. She poured no water for me, yet I spend the whole day drinking [in the sight of her beauty]. As my soul lives, O beloved one, may you cause me to be brought into your presence. . . . Come, that you may spend the day in merriment, day after day for three days, sitting in my shade. Her lover is at her right side. She makes him drunk, yielding to his request. . . . But [no matter what I see her do] I am discreet to tell not what I see. I will speak no word."

performing a back bend (the finest of these appears on an ostrakon in Turin's Egyptian Museum); a group of girls leaning back with one leg on the ground and the other in a high-kick; girls lifting or throwing one another or performing somersaults and the like. In other depictions there is true dancing with elegant leg-movements and charming gestures, with torsos bending and heads inclined as rhythm required.[66]

Another interesting feature of the Egyptian dancers depicted in paintings is their attire. They most often wore skirts or tunics that were partially open in front, which allowed for revealing flashes of skin while they were dancing. That modesty was not a significant factor is also apparent from paintings showing women dancing naked, except for a decorative band or ribbon worn around the hips or waist. The paintings also carefully depict dancers' well-defined muscles, suggesting that they were professionals who trained hard and performed often. Along with musicians, potters, stonemasons, jewelry makers, painters, scribes, and other skilled artists and professionals, they added a layer of culture, sophistication, and pleasure to life in one of the greatest civilized centers of the ancient world.

Notes

Introduction: The Structured Lives of Egyptian Craftsmen

1. Joyce Tyldesley, *Ramesses: Egypt's Greatest Pharaoh.* New York: Penguin, 2000, p. 54.
2. Ian Shaw and Paul Nicholson, *The Dictionary of Ancient Egypt.* New York: Harry N. Abrams, 1995, pp. 38–39.
3. A. Rosalie David, *Handbook to Life in Ancient Egypt.* New York: Facts On File, 1998, p. 180.
4. James F. Romano, *Daily Life of the Ancient Egyptians.* Pittsburgh: Carnegie Museum of Natural History, 1990, pp. 2, 38.

Chapter 1: Artistry in Stone

5. Modern scholars differ widely on the dating of this and other time periods for ancient Egypt, and a number of alternate chronologies are in use. For example, some experts date the end of the Neolithic Age to 5500 B.C., others to 5000 B.C., and still others to as late as 4000 B.C., depending on their application of varying criteria. All dates cited in this book follow one of the more widely accepted dating schemes.
6. Eugen Strouhal, *Life of the Ancient Egyptians.* Norman: University of Oklahoma Press, 1992, p. 139.
7. Lionel Casson, *Everyday Life in Ancient Egypt.* Baltimore: Johns Hopkins University Press, 2001, p. 69.
8. Dieter Arnold, *Building in Egypt: Pharaonic Stone Masonry.* Oxford, England: Oxford University Press, 1991, pp. 45, 257.
9. Jaromir Malek, *Egyptian Art.* London: Phaidon, 1999, p. 132.
10. Manuel Robbins, *The Collapse of the Bronze Age: The Story of Greece, Troy, Israel, Egypt, and the Peoples of the Sea.* San Jose, CA: Authors Choice, 2001, pp. 29–30.
11. Gay Robins, *Egyptian Statues.* Buckinghamshire, England: Shire, 2003, pp. 9–10.

Chapter 2: Production of Pottery and Glass

12. Quoted in Strouhal, *Life of the Ancient Egyptians,* p. 141.
13. Strouhal, *Life of the Ancient Egyptians,* p. 141.
14. David, *Handbook,* pp. 286–87.
15. Shaw and Nicholson, *Dictionary of Ancient Egypt,* p. 113.

Chapter 3: Cloth Making and Leather Working

16. David, *Handbook,* p. 290.

17. Quoted in Strouhal, *Life of the Ancient Egyptians,* p. 148.
18. Strouhal, *Life of the Ancient Egyptians,* p. 148.
19. David, *Handbook,* p. 294.

Chapter 4: Working with Metal and Wood

20. Quoted in T.G.H. James, *Pharaoh's People: Scenes from Life in Imperial Egypt.* New York: Tauris Parke, 2003, p. 204.
21. James, *Pharaoh's People,* p. 204.
22. Quoted in Casson, *Everyday Life,* p. 71.
23. Quoted in Karl Muller, *Geographi Graeci Minores.* Hildesheim, Germany: G. Olms, 1990, pp. 124–27.
24. Strouhal, *Life of the Ancient Egyptians,* p. 151.
25. David, *Handbook,* pp. 303–304.
26. James, *Pharaoh's People,* p. 235.

Chapter 5: Jewelry Making and Painting

27. David, *Handbook,* p. 308.
28. Malek, *Egyptian Art,* pp. 203–204.
29. Romano, *Daily Life,* p. 17.
30. Malek, *Egyptian Art,* pp. 249–51.

Chapter 6: Writing and Literature

31. Quoted in J.H. Breasted, ed., *Ancient Records of Egypt.* 5 vols. New York: Russell and Russell, 1962, vol. 3, pp. 77–78.
32. Quoted in James B. Pritchard, ed., *Ancient Near Eastern Texts Relating to the Old Testament.* Princeton, NJ: Princeton University Press, 1969, p. 20.
33. Pliny the Elder, *Natural History,* excerpted in *Natural History: A Selection,* trans. John F. Healy. New York: Penguin, 1991, pp. 176–77.
34. David, *Handbook,* p. 203.
35. Quoted in Josephine Mayer and Tom Prideaux, eds., *Never to Die: The Egyptians in Their Own Words.* New York: Viking, 1938, pp. 42–44.
36. Quoted in Miriam Lichtheim, ed., *Ancient Egyptian Literature: A Book of Readings.* 2 vols. Berkeley and Los Angeles: University of California Press, 1975–1976, vol. 2, p. 125.
37. Quoted in Pritchard, *Ancient Near Eastern Texts,* pp. 370–71.
38. Quoted in Breasted, *Ancient Records,* vol. 2, p. 183.
39. Quoted in W.K. Simpson, ed., *The Literature of Ancient Egypt: An Anthology of Stories, Instructions, and Poetry.* New Haven, CT: Yale University Press, 1973, pp. 160, 162.

Chapter 7: Leisure Games and Sports

40. Edith Hamilton, *The Greek Way to Western Civilization.* New York: New American Library, 1930, pp. 18–19.
41. Quoted in Vera Olivova, *Sports and Games in the Ancient World.* New York: St. Martin's, 1984, p. 43.
42. Olivova, *Sports and Games,* pp. 45, 48.
43. Shaw and Nicholson, *Dictionary of Ancient Egypt,* p. 107.
44. Quoted in Olivova, *Sports and Games,* pp. 51–52.
45. Quoted in Olivova, *Sports and Games,* p. 51.

46. Seneca, *Natural Questions*, excerpted in C.D.N. Costa, trans. and ed., *Seneca: Dialogues and Letters*. New York: Penguin, 1997, p. 110.

47. Seneca, *Natural Questions*, in Costa, *Seneca*, pp. 110–11.

48. Quoted in Michael B. Poliakoff, *Combat Sports in the Ancient World*. New Haven, CT: Yale University Press, 1987, p. 27.

49. Quoted in Gerald W. Morton and George M. O'Brien, *Wrestling to Rasslin: Ancient Sport to American Spectacle*. Bowling Green, OH: Bowling Green State University Press, 1985, p. 7.

Chapter 8: Hunting and Fishing

50. Herodotus, *The Histories*, trans. Aubrey de Sélincourt. New York: Penguin, 1972, p. 143.

51. Strouhal, *Life of the Ancient Egyptians*, p. 117.

52. Quoted in Olivova, *Sports and Games*, p. 49.

53. Quoted in Casson, *Everyday Life*, p. 49.

54. Quoted in Strouhal, *Life of the Ancient Egyptians*, p. 123.

55. Strouhal, *Life of the Ancient Egyptians*, p. 123.

56. Quoted in Strouhal, *Life of the Ancient Egyptians*, p. 123.

57. Herodotus, *Histories*, p. 155.

Chapter 9: Music, Singing, and Dancing

58. Strouhal, *Life of the Ancient Egyptians*, p. 44.

59. Herodotus, *Histories*, p. 143.

60. Quoted in Mayer and Prideaux, *Never to Die*, p. 47.

61. Quoted in Mayer and Prideaux, *Never to Die*, p. 96.

62. Quoted in Simpson, *Literature of Ancient Egypt*, p. 282.

63. Quoted in Breasted, *Ancient Records*, vol. 3, pp. 263–64. Incidentally, this inscription is the earliest known reference in literature to the ancient kingdom of Israel. For more on this topic, see Breasted's comments on pp. 257–59.

64. Quoted in Simpson, *Literature of Ancient Egypt*, p. 298.

65. Quoted in Simpson, *Literature of Ancient Egypt*, p. 303.

66. Strouhal, *Life of the Ancient Egyptians*, p. 42.

Chronology

General Time Periods of Ancient Egypt (as formulated by modern scholars)

B.C.

ca. 9000–5500
Approximate years of Egypt's Neolithic Age (or New Stone Age), before the advent of towns and states, during which tools and weapons are made exclusively from stone.

ca. 5500–3100
Years of Egypt's so-called Predynastic Period, during which the country is divided into many small city-states and eventually into two major kingdoms—Upper Egypt and Lower Egypt.

ca. 3100–2686
Years of the Early Dynastic Period, encompassing the reigns of the nine rulers of the First Dynasty and seven rulers of the Second Dynasty.

ca. 2686–2181
Years of the Old Kingdom (encompassing the rulers of the Third, Fourth, Fifth, and Sixth dynasties), during which most of Egypt's pyramids are built, including the largest ones, at Giza (near modern Cairo).

ca. 2181–2055
Years of the First Intermediate Period, which witnesses much civil strife and a partial breakdown of central authority and law and order.

ca. 2055–1650
Years of the Middle Kingdom (encompassing the Eleventh, Twelfth, Thirteenth, and Fourteenth dynasties), in which the Egyptians begin expanding their territory by conquest and their wealth through trade.

ca. 1650–1550
Years of the Second Intermediate Period, also called the Hyksos period in reference to an Asiatic people of that name who invade and occupy Egypt.

ca. 1550–1069
Years of the New Kingdom (encompassing the Eighteenth, Nineteenth, and Twentieth dynasties), in which a series of vigorous pharaohs create an Egyptian empire and erect numerous large temples, palaces, and forts.

ca. 1069–747
Years of the Third Intermediate Period, in which Egypt falls into steady military, political, and cultural decline.

ca. 747–332
Years of the Late Period, during most of which members of foreign-born dynasties rule Egypt.

332–30
Years of the Ptolemaic Period (or Egypt's Greek Period), during which Ptolemy and his descendants rule Egypt.

30 B.C.–A.D. 395
Years of the Roman Period, in which a series of Roman emperors control Egypt.

Glossary

alloy: A mixture of two or more metals.

amulet: An object, either worn or carried, thought to have magical properties that would protect the owner.

antiquity: Ancient times.

aulos: A double flute imported into Egypt from Greece during the Late Period or Ptolemaic Period.

bedjty: A metalsmith.

brass: A mixture of the metals copper and zinc.

bronze: A mixture of the metals copper and tin.

canons of proportion: General rules and measurements that artists and sculptors used to ensure that they portrayed the human body and other subjects correctly.

cartouche: In ancient Egypt, an oval or oblong object or figure that held an inscription, picture, or both.

coarse ware (or **Nile silt ware**): Simple, inexpensive pottery made from local Egyptian silt and clay.

colossi: Giant statues.

demotic: A written script that developed in Egypt in the Late Period.

electrum: A mixture of gold and silver.

faience: A glistening substance made from crushed quartz that the Egyptians used widely in the production of pottery and jewelry.

flax: Plant that grows widely in Egypt and from which cloth was made.

frontalism: A common artistic convention in which a human body is portrayed with the head and legs in profile but the eye and upper body facing forward (or frontally).

gesso: A painting medium consisting of a sort of plaster made from powdered chalk.

hieratic: A form of writing that developed in Early Dynastic Egypt.

hieroglyphics: A system of picture writing, including the one developed in Egypt in the late 3000s B.C.

hydraulos: A large organ powered by a bellows, invented by an Alexandrian Greek in the Ptolemaic Period.

kedu: Potters or mud-brick makers.

knapping: Chipping a stone, usually to sharpen it.

mehen: A board game referred to as the "snake game," the rules of which are now unclear.

monumental: Large-scale, a term usually used to describe large buildings.

ostrakon (plural, **ostraca**): A piece of broken pottery.

papyrus (plural, **papyri**): A water plant that grows widely in Egypt, or a kind of paper made from the papyrus plant.

pectoral: A large, ornamented necklace worn by the well-to-do in ancient Egypt.

register: A horizontal band or panel of paintings or sculptures on a wall, vase, or some other surface.

relief (or **bas-relief**): A three-dimensional carving raised from a flat surface.

scarab: An amulet or some other object in the shape of a scarab beetle.

senet: A popular game that used a game board with thirty squares and a number of game pieces that were moved on the board.

sesh: Painters who filled in the outlines created by sketch artists known as *sesh kedut*.

sistrum: A native Egyptian musical instrument consisting of a handheld rattle with small cymbal-like metal disks attached.

stela (plural **stelae**): A slab of stone or wood used as a marker or monument.

tawing: A leather-making process consisting of rubbing an animal hide with alum.

tjebu: Leather workers.

tjehenet: Faience.

udjat: An amulet or other object that portrayed the Eye of Horus, a religious symbol thought to have magical properties.

vizier: A pharaoh's chief administrator and adviser.

warp and weft: The orientation of the threads during weaving; the warp threads were the vertical ones, the weft threads the horizontal ones.

wesekh: A broad band of beads or other decorations worn like a necklace.

For Further Reading

Books

Lionel Casson, *Everyday Life in Ancient Egypt.* Baltimore: Johns Hopkins University Press, 2001. An excellent, fascinating examination of ancient Egyptian life by a great scholar. (The reading level is high school and general adult.)

Judith Crosher, *Technology in the Time of Ancient Egypt.* New York: Raintree, 1998. A general look at the building tools and labor-saving devices available to the ancient Egyptians.

Ruthie Knapp and Janice Lehmberg, *Egyptian Art.* New York: Sterling, 1998. A well-written introduction to the subject, with several colorful illustrations.

Joyce Milton and Charles Micucci, *Hieroglyphs.* New York: Grosset and Dunlap, 2000. This introduction to the picture signs of ancient Egyptian writing is well organized and easy to read.

Jane Shuter, *Builders and Craftsmen of Ancient Egypt.* Crystal Lake, IL: Heinemann Library, 1998. A well-written general examination of ancient Egyptian builders and artisans.

Web Sites

Ancient Egyptian Furniture and Woodworking (www.geocities.com/gpkillen.) An excellent site created by noted English scholar Geoffrey Killen, with several links to related topics.

Ancient Egyptian Papyrus (www.mnsu. edu/emuseum/prehistory/egypt/ dailylife/papyrus.html.) A brief overview of the making and use of ancient papyrus, the paper on which the Egyptians and other ancients wrote literature.

Egyptian Painting (www.mnsu.edu/ emuseum/prehistory/egypt/artisans/pain ting.htm.) A useful general introduction to the subject, with references and links to other Internet sites.

Play in Ancient Egypt (http://nefertiti. iwebland.com/timelines/topics/games. htm.) Discusses children's games, toys, and board games. This site is part of a larger and very useful collection of links about ancient Egyptian culture.

Works Consulted

Major Works

Cyril Aldred, *Egyptian Art*. London: Thames and Hudson, 1980. One of the most informative general studies of the subject.

W.V. Davies, *Egyptian Hieroglyphics*. Berkeley and Los Angeles: University of California Press, 1987. A well-written synopsis of Egyptian picture writing that also includes an informative section on its decipherment.

Manfred Decker, *Sports and Games in Ancient Egypt*. New Haven, CT: Yale University Press, 1992. This well-organized and well-researched volume examines all of the major evidence for leisure activities in ancient Egypt.

Sergio Donadoni, ed., *The Egyptians*. Trans. Robert Bianchi et al. Chicago: University of Chicago Press, 1990. Contains a series of long essays by noted scholars, including an informative one on ancient Egyptian craftsmen.

T.G.H. James, *Pharaoh's People: Scenes from Life in Imperial Egypt*. New York: Tauris Parke, 2003. The author goes into considerable detail on aspects of ancient Egyptian society that normally receive less attention, including literacy and the contributions of metalsmiths and carpenters.

T.G.H. James and W.V. Davies, *Egyptian Sculpture*. Cambridge, MA: Harvard University Press, 1983. An excellent overview of the creation of statues and other sculpted artifacts in ancient Egypt.

Geoffrey Killen, *Egyptian Woodworking and Furniture*. Princes Risborough, England: Shire, 1994. The most comprehensive concise study of ancient Egyptian woodworkers and their craft.

Jaromir Malek, *Egyptian Art*. London: Phaidon, 1999. A fine general synopsis of the subject, broken down in a chronological sequence.

Lise Manniche, *Music and Musicians in Ancient Egypt*. London: Dover, 1992. Discusses the musical instruments in use in ancient Egypt and what is known about the social status and lives of the musicians themselves.

Gay Robins, *Egyptian Painting and Relief*. Princes Risborough, England: Shire, 1986. A noted scholar of ancient Egypt, Robins delivers a thorough summary of one of the most important crafts in that society.

———, *Egyptian Statues*. Buckinghamshire, England: Shire, 2003. Another fine scholarly study by Robins, this one discusses the styles, functions, and making of ancient Egyptian statues.

Bernd Scheel, *Egyptian Metalworking and Tools*. Princes Risborough, England: Shire, 1989. A well-written and very informative overview of the art of metalworking in ancient Egypt.

David P. Silverman, ed., *Ancient Egypt*. New York: Oxford University Press, 1997. A very useful general depiction of ancient Egyptian culture, with large sections on art, architecture, and writing.

Eugen Strouhal, *Life of the Ancient Egyptians*. Norman: University of Oklahoma Press, 1992. One of the best recent general studies of ancient Egyptian life, this one features several extended discussions of various craftsmen and artists.

Other Important Works

Primary Sources

J.H. Breasted, ed., *Ancient Records of Egypt*. 5 vols. New York: Russell and Russell, 1962.

C.D.N. Costa, trans. and ed., *Seneca: Dialogues and Letters*. New York: Penguin, 1997.

A.H. Gardiner, "The Treaty of Alliance Between Hattusilis, King of the Hittites, and the Pharaoh Ramesses II of Egypt," *Journal of Egyptian Archaeology*, vol. 6, 1920.

Herodotus, *The Histories*. Trans. Aubrey de Sélincourt. New York: Penguin, 1972.

Miriam Lichtheim, ed., *Ancient Egyptian Literature: A Book of Readings*. 2 vols. Berkeley and Los Angeles: University of California Press, 1975–1976.

Josephine Mayer and Tom Prideaux, eds., *Never to Die: The Egyptians in Their Own Words*. New York: Viking, 1938.

Karl Muller, *Geographi Graeci Minores*. Hildesheim, Germany: G. Olms, 1990.

Pliny the Elder, *Natural History*, excerpted in *Natural History: A Selection*. Trans. John F. Healy. New York: Penguin, 1991.

James B. Pritchard, ed., *Ancient Near Eastern Texts Relating to the Old Testament*. Princeton, NJ: Princeton University Press, 1969.

W.K. Simpson, ed., *The Literature of Ancient Egypt: An Anthology of Stories, Instructions, and Poetry*. New Haven, CT: Yale University Press, 1973.

Modern Sources

Carol Andrews, *Ancient Egyptian Jewelry*. London: British Museum, 1996.

Dieter Arnold, *Building in Egypt: Pharaonic Stone Masonry*. Oxford, England: Oxford University Press, 1991.

Paul G. Bahn, ed., *The Cambridge Illustrated History of Archaeology*. New York: Cambridge University Press, 1996.

Douglas J. Brewer and Renee R. Freidman, *Fish and Fishing in Ancient Egypt*. Warminster, England: Aris and Phillips, 1990.

Lionel Casson, *Ancient Egypt*. New York: Random House, 1983.

A. Rosalie David, *Handbook to Life in Ancient Egypt*. New York: Facts On File, 1998.

Nicolas Grimal, *A History of Ancient Egypt*. Trans. Ian Shaw. Oxford, England: Blackwell, 1992.

Edith Hamilton, *The Greek Way to Western Civilization*. New York: New American Library, 1930.

Jill Kamil, *The Ancient Egyptians: Life in the Old Kingdom*. Cairo, Egypt: American University in Cairo Press, 1996.

Alfred Lucas and J.R. Harris, *Ancient Egyptian Materials and Industries*. Mineola, NY: Dover, 1999.

A.G. McDowell, *Village Life in Ancient Egypt.* New York: Oxford University Press, 1999.

Gerald W. Morton and George M. O'Brien, *Wrestling to Rasslin: Ancient Sport to American Spectacle.* Bowling Green, OH: Bowling Green State University Press, 1985.

Vera Olivova, *Sports and Games in the Ancient World.* New York: St. Martin's, 1984.

Michael B. Poliakoff, *Combat Sports in the Ancient World.* New Haven, CT: Yale University Press, 1987.

Manuel Robbins, *The Collapse of the Bronze Age: The Story of Greece, Troy, Israel, Egypt, and the Peoples of the Sea.* San Jose, CA: Authors Choice, 2001.

James F. Romano, *Daily Life of the Ancient Egyptians.* Pittsburgh: Carnegie Museum of Natural History, 1990.

Ian Shaw and Paul Nicholson, *The Dictionary of Ancient Egypt.* New York: Harry N. Abrams, 1995.

William S. Smith et al., *The Art and Architecture of Ancient Egypt.* New Haven, CT: Yale University Press, 1999.

Joyce Tyldesley, *Ramesses: Egypt's Greatest Pharaoh.* New York: Penguin, 2000.

Index

Picture Credits

Cover, Lawrence Alma-Tadema's The Egyptian Chess Players/Bridgeman Art Library

Akg-Images, 62, 80, 86, 94

Akg-Images/Francois Gue'net, 36

Akg-Images/Andrea Jemolo, 85

Akg-Images/Gilles Mermet, 9, 52

Art Archive/Dagli Orti, 18, 33(top), 43, 61

Art Archive/Egypt Museum, Cairo/Dagli Orti, 30, 34, 54(bottom)

Art Archive/Musee de Louvre, Paris/Dagli Orti, 27, 54(top)

Art Archive/Pharaonic Village, Cairo/Dagli Orti, 47

Art Renewal .org, 88

Borromeo/Art Resource, N.Y., 24

Werner Forman/Art Resource, N.Y., 28, 82

Giraudon/Art Resource, N.Y., 14, 28, 65

HIP/Art Resource, N.Y., 63, 71(right)

Erich Lessing/Art Resource, N.Y., 25, 39, 45, 48, 56, 57, 76, 81

Scala/Art Resource, N.Y., 50, 71(left), 84

Vanni/Art Resource, N.Y., 68

© Bettman/CORBIS, 22

© Werner Forman/CORBIS, 90

© Charles and Josette Lenars/CORBIS, 58

© Gianni Dagli Orti/CORBIS, 33(bottom), 40, 73(both), 74

© Carl and Ann Purcell/CORBIS, 13

© Stapleton Collection/CORBIS, 19, 91

© Sandro Vanni/CORBIS, 64

© Roger Wood/CORBIS, 10, 31

Corel, 20

About the Author

Historian and award-winning writer Don Nardo has written or edited numerous books about the ancient world, including *Empires of Mesopotamia, The Ancient Greeks, Life of a Roman Gladiator, The Etruscans, Ancient Civilizations,* and the *Greenhaven Encyclopedia of Greek and Roman Mythology.* Mr. Nardo lives with his wife, Christine, in Massachusetts.